# Pakistan Army
## Modernisation, Arms Procurement and Capacity Building

# Pakistan Army
## Modernisation, Arms Procurement and Capacity Building

**Dr Shah Alam**

**Vij Books India Pvt Ltd**
New Delhi, India

Published   by

**Vij Books India Pvt Ltd**
(Publishers, Distributors & Importers)
2/19, Ansari Road, Darya Ganj
New Delhi - 110002
Phones: 91-11-43596460, 91-11-47340674
Fax: 91-11-47340674
e-mail  : vijbooks@rediffmail.com
web: www.vijbooks.com

# Contents

# List of Tables

# Preface

Pakistan emerged with India's partition in 1947. The newly created state felt need for strong armed forces to secure borders and meet external challenges. Pakistan initiated military modernisation programme to meet defence needs. Military modernisation largely depends on the country's financial strength and the ability to make strategic alliances. Financial and industrial constraints are elements that had forceful impact on Pakistan's armed forces modernisation policy. Initially, the Pakistan Army had faced the challenges of shortage of manpower, assets, arms and finance. However, Pakistan's military capability grew, despite numerous challenges. Particularly, the Army grew more rapidly than the Air Force and Navy.

Gen Ayub Khan took measures to establish defence production industry in the country and was continued by the successive regimes. Prime Minister Zulfiqar Ali Bhutto put emphasis in establishing the arms production industry that was continued by the Zia regime. Pakistan took foreign assistance in establishing defence production industry, but achieved partial success in producing arms of its own. Pakistan continued to rely on foreign arms suppliers for its army and other services because of industrial and financial constraints.

Pakistan's relations with the US had passed through ups and downs and the two countries could not maintain a long stable relationship and 'irritants' continued. The US sought to continue its relations with Pakistan due to its strategic location and some other reasons. Pakistan was in the quest for security and needed financial assistance and arms from the US and the West, to bolster its security. In order to bolster its security, Pakistan signed security and defence pacts with the US and entered into the US/West-sponsored security pacts. The event had changed the direction of Pakistan, and that of the Pakistan Army. However, Pakistan continued to face challenges in modernising its Army.

Pakistan-US warm relations in the 1950s and Pakistan's defence and security pacts with the US and the West facilitated the flows of funds and arms to Pakistan. But, the flow of arms and funds to Pakistan did not continue in the 1960s as in the 1950s. The US and Britain imposed arms supply embargo on Pakistan in the event of India-Pakistan war 1965. The event brought a turning point in Pakistan's arms acquisitions policy and the Eastern bloc assumed a significant place for obtaining arms. Beijing supplied arms to Islamabad during the India-Pakistan war 1965 and continued that. In the 1970s, China supplied tanks, in bulk, to Pakistan, that played a significant role in modernising and strengthening the Army. China supplied not only arms to Pakistan but also assisted in establishing defence production industry. China's arms transfer policy to Pakistan indicates the convergence of views between the two countries on regional security.

Pakistan-US relation was not warm in the 1970s. As a result, Islamabad received few arms from Washington. The US and the West resumed arms supply to Pakistan in the 1980s, in the event of the Soviet military intervention in Afghanistan, in 1979. Pakistan received arms and funds in bulk from the US and the West in the 1980s but the momentum did not continue in the 1990s. However, the Pakistan Army grew substantially and comprehensively in the 1980s because of the flow of the US and the West funds and arms to Pakistan. The US again supplied arms to Pakistan, post-September 2001. Pakistan obtained tanks and other arms from Russia, Belarus and Ukraine in the 1990s and onwards. Pakistan's arms acquisition policy helped in expanding and modernising the army. Command and control structure of the Pakistan Army improved too.

China had been playing a significant role in expanding, developing and modernising the Pakistan Army with supplying arms since the 1960s. China supplied not only tanks and arms in bulk to Pakistan, but also assisted in establishing the defence industrial complex. China had played a significant role in establishing and expanding Pakistan's defence industrial base. Beijing supplied nuclear-related material and technologies to Islamabad and missiles and missile-related technologies as well. Pakistan-China complex relationship and Beijing's arms transfer policy towards Islamabad added intricacies in the regional security.

The Pakistan Army has considerably improved but still carries shortcomings. Pakistan's dependency on external arms suppliers will be continuing because of financial and industrial constraints. These factors are major challenges in the modernisation process of the Pakistan Army. Nonetheless, Pakistan will continue modernisation of the Army, with inducting new and sophisticated arms and improving command and control system.

This book undertakes the Pakistan Army's genesis, development, modernisation, arms procurement, command and control, and decision-making process. The study explains and analyses the Pakistan Army's expansion, development and modernisation process that began in the 1950s and continued, despite several obstacles. Pakistan received arms, technology and funds from abroad, for its Army. The foreign countries had played the crucial role in the modernisation drive of the Pakistan Army. The book examines the relationship between the recipient and the suppliers and their dynamics.

Dr Shah Alam

New Delhi
December 2011

# Abbreviations and Acronyms

| | |
|---|---|
| AFRC | Armed Forces Reconstitution Committee |
| AG | Adjutant General |
| APC | Armoured Personnel Carrier |
| ARC | Army Reserve Central |
| ARN | Army Reserve North |
| ARS | Army Reserve South |
| ARV | Armoured Recovery Vehicle |
| ATM | Anti-tank Missile |
| CENTO | Central Treaty Organisation |
| CGS | Chief of General Staff |
| C-in-C | Commander-in-Chief |
| CLS | Chief of Logistics Staff |
| COAS | Chief of Army Staff |
| COS | Chief of Staff |
| DCC | Defence Committee of the Cabinet |
| UNO | United Nations Organisation |
| USSR | United Soviet Socialist Republic |
| DMT | Directorate of Military Training |
| FATA | Federally Administered Tribal Areas |
| FF | Frontier Forces |
| GHQ | General Headquarters |
| GOC | General Officer Commanding |

| | |
|---|---|
| HIT | Heavy Industry Taxila |
| HRF | Heavy Rebuild Factory |
| HQ | Headquarters |
| IGT&E | Inspector General of Training and Evaluation |
| IISS | International Institute for Strategic Studies |
| IMA | Indian Military Academy |
| IOP | Institute of Optronics |
| ISI | Inter Services Intelligence |
| JAG | Judge Advocate General |
| JCSC | Joint Chiefs of Staff Committee |
| LOC | Line of Control |
| MBT | Main Battle Tank |
| ME | Margalla Electronics |
| MES | Military Engineering Service |
| MS | Military Secretary |
| NATO | North Atlantic Treaty Organisation |
| NWFP | North West Frontier Province |
| PAC | Pakistan Aeronautical Complex |
| PACO | Pakistan Automobile Corporation |
| PMA | Pakistan Military Academy |
| POFs | Pakistan Ordnance Factories |
| POWs | Prisoner of Wars |
| PSO's | Principal Staff Officers |
| QMG | Quartermaster General |
| Recce | Reconnaissance (air craft or vehicle) |
| RIAS | Royal Indian Army Service Corps |

| | |
|---|---|
| SA | Surface-to-Air Missile |
| SEATO | South East Asia Treaty Organisation |
| SF | Security Forces |
| SPH | Self-propelled Howitzer |
| SSM | Surface-to-Surface Missile |
| TG | Towed Gun |
| TH | Towed Howitzer |
| TML | Trans-Mobile Limited |
| UAE | United Arab Emirate |
| UNO | United Nations Organisation |
| USSR | United Soviet Socialist Republic |

# Pakistan Army

## Chief of Army Staffs (COAS)

| S. No. | Name of Army Chief | Period |
|--------|--------------------|--------|
| 1 | Gen Sir Frank Messervy | August 1947- February 1948 |
| 2 | Gen Sir Duglas Gracey | February 1948- January 1951 |
| 3 | Gen Mohammad Ayub Khan | January 1951- October 1958 |
| 4 | Gen Mohammad Musa Khan | October 1951-September 1966 |
| 5 | Gen A M Yahya Khan | September 1966-December 1671 |
| 6 | Gen Gul Hasan | December 1971-March 1972 |
| 7 | Gen Takka Khan | March 1972-March 1976 |
| 8 | Gen Mohammad Zia-Ul-Haq | March 1976-August 1988 |
| 9 | Gen Mirza Aslam Beg | August 1988-August 1991 |
| 10 | Gen Asif Nawaz | August 1991- January 1993 |
| 11 | Gen Aabdul Waheed | January 1993- January 1996 |
| 12 | Gen Jehangir Karamat | January 1996- October 1998 |
| 13 | Gen Pervez Musharraf | October 1998- November 2007 |
| 14 | Gen Ashfaq Pervez Kayani | November 2007 |

# 1

# Introduction

The Pakistan Armed Forces emerged with the division of the British Indian Armed Forces in 1947. The birth of the Pakistan Army is associated with the emergence of the Pakistan Armed Forces. From the very beginning, Pakistan started to procure arms from abroad and tried to maintain a balance between the arms and fighting forces. The Pakistan Army was expanded and modernised with induction of weapons. Historical experiences, memories of wars and Pakistan's adversarial relations with India have shaped the strategic culture of Pakistan. The strategic culture that emerged, contributed in shaping, building and reorganising the Pakistan Army. The modernisation process began during the Ayub period and was continued by the successive regimes. The memories of wars and humiliating defeats were instrumental in sustaining the military build-up of Pakistan.

Pakistan's military capability grew over a period of time. Particularly, the Army grew far more rapidly in comparison to the Air Force and the Navy. The Pakistan Army employed resources in its expansion and modernisation. The arms acquisitions policy was pursued by the Army that continued. Post-1965, Pakistan diversified weapons procurement sources. A country's military capability is dependent upon the linkage between available arms and its strategic options. The availability of weapons, provides options to a country, for exercising its power. Moreover, the availability of weapons, increases the manoeuvring capacity of a country.

## Threat perception

In Pakistan's perception, India and Afghanistan are main threats to its security. Pakistan categorises India as a 'primary threat' and Afghanistan as a 'secondary threat' to its security. The two countries are perceived by Pakistan, as its threats. Pakistan's hostile relations with India and Afghanistan have influenced the shaping of its strategic culture. The Pakistan Armed Forces are the product of the emerging strategic culture of Pakistan. The Pakistan Army is being developed to meet security challenges.

Pakistan's adversarial relations with India play a vital role in the formation of its official threat perception and national security plans. Pakistan's greatest concern, since 1947, has been to find means to thwart India, to gain an important place in the region. The Soviet intervention in Afghanistan, in 1979, was interpreted as a threat to Pakistan. But the fact remains that even after 1979, Pakistan continued to consider India as a 'primary threat'.

For Pakistan, India has remained the primary concern. This attitude is rooted in the mistrust, that resulted from the experience of the partition in 1947. Developments at the time of partition created mistrust that still exists. The military regimes and political governments operating under the influence of the Armed Forces, have resorted to displaying a tough military posture against India, for the purposes of acquiring political legitimacy. The vested interests ensured the creating of tensions for their political, personal and organisational gains. Tensions between India and Pakistan grew markedly during the 1980s and 1990s. Pakistan's hostile attitude towards India, led to strengthen weapon acquisition demand of the Army. Pakistan's military programme is closely tied with India's. Pakistan's efforts to maintain conventional balance and its decision, in 1998, to conduct nuclear tests after India, not only reflects Islamabad's sense of insecurity but also the fact that it seeks parity with India. However, the Pakistan Army will remain smaller than the Indian Army.

The containment of India has always been the corner-stone of Pakistan's strategic perspective. The sense of insecurity is further deepened by the fragmentation of the Pakistani society – rise of Islamic fundamentalism, religious terrorism, sectarian conflict, ethnic conflict, insurgency and problems in Baluchistan. The civil society of Pakistan is divided on ethnic, religious, sectarian, linguistic, and regional grounds.

In Pakistan's perception, Afghanistan is a threat, but not as much of a threat as India poses. Strategically, Afghanistan is a 'secondary threat' and a source of concern for Pakistan. This notion received impetus with the Soviet intervention in Afghanistan, in 1979. The fragile political atmosphere of Afghanistan, in 1979 and the Soviet intervention, alarmed Pakistan. The Soviet intervention of Afghanistan, added a new dimension to Pakistan's threat perception. Pakistan's Afghan policy, pursued in the early 1980s, was a continuation of its earlier policy, that viewed Afghanistan as a country inimical to Pakistan's security interests. The threat Afghanistan posed to Pakistan, however, was not comparable to that of India. The Soviet military intervention in Afghanistan was seen as a potential threat. The impact of the Soviet intervention in Afghanistan was witnessed on the Pakistan-US relations.

Gen Zia formulated plans for Afghanistan. He hoped to use Afghanistan, to provide strategic depth to Pakistan. Therefore, he sought the help of the Mujahidin, in a prospective conflict with India, which included the presence of the Pakistani intelligence services network in Afghanistan. It did not happen. He was not happy with the outcome of the Geneva Accord, that allowed the Soviet Union to withdraw, without forming a pro-Pakistan government in Afghanistan, but he pursued his plans and his successors in the Army continued that.[1] The involvement of the Pakistan Army, grew in Afghanistan, in the 1980s.

Pakistan sought to acquire US military and economic aid that was only possible through convergence of views between the two countries. This opportunity presented itself to Pakistan in the 1980s, while the US was searching for an ally in the South Asia, to contain the growing influence of the Soviet Union. Like the 1950s and 1960s, the US military hardware was transferred in bulk, to Pakistan. The Regan Administration agreed to strengthen Pakistan, through arms transfers and economic aid. Weapons were transferred, thus was a major factor in formulating Pakistan's offensive posture, towards the Soviet Union. Considering Islamabad's hostile relations with New Delhi, these arms gave Pakistan the ability to stand up against

---

[1] Ayesha Siddiqa-Agha, *Pakistan's Arms Procurement and Military Buildup, 1979-99: In Search of a Policy* (New York: Palgrave, 2001), p. 101

India, as had happened in 1965.[2] The 1965 India-Pakistan War led to the US arms supply embargo on both the South Asian countries, but Pakistan was the most affected, because its dependence upon the US arms was greater than that of India.[3] India-Soviet Union close links, the Soviet intervention in Afghanistan, and Pakistan's hostility with India, was perceived in Pakistan, as a security threat.

In the 1980s, the Pakistan-US warm relationship, facilitated the transfer of weapons to the Pakistan Army. The modern arms transferred to Pakistan, contributed in the expansion and modernisation of the Pakistan Army. Pakistan received tanks and other weapons to fight against the Soviet intervention. However, this warm relationship did not continue in the 1990s in the same way that the two countries enjoyed, in the 1980s. With the beginning of the Soviet withdrawal from Afghanistan in 1988, Pakistan did not remain a valuable strategic asset for the US. Pakistan did not remain a strategic ally in the US defence and foreign policy planning. Pakistan's relevance for the US policy-making, reduced. Moreover, the disintegration of the Soviet Union in 1991, further eroded relevancy of Pakistan, for the US.

Pakistan-US relations reached the lowest ebb, in the early 1990s. However, joint commando exercises were held several times, from 1990 to 1997, but with limited objectives. The idea was to maintain a certain level of confidence in the Pakistani administration and in its links with the US, without creating any liabilities for Washington. Pakistan desired for a permanent military alignment with the US and made efforts for that. Pakistan always needed a foreign source, that could be used as a cover to bolster its own credibility and strength, while negotiating or dealing with India.[4] In the 1950s, Pakistan was characterised as a large and strategically pivotal country. Pakistan had achieved this status largely through its alliance with the US and membership in the SEATO and Baghdad Pact/CENTO and these led to a flow of weapons and high levels of training and proficiency.[5]

---

[2] Ibid., p. 14

[3] Ibid

[4] Ibid., p. 100

[5] Stephen P Cohen, *The Pakistan Army 1998 Edition* (Karachi: Oxford University Press, 1998), p. 10

But by 1972, Pakistan was ruined and its Army was defeated.

Pakistan Army's intoxication with its own mythology, excessive confidence in its strategic attractiveness to outside powers, poor technology, etc. led to the country's permanent strategic inferiority, made it increasingly dependent upon other states and eventually even these grew more unreliable.[6] Pakistan continued to remain dependent on foreign sources, for arms and ammunitions. The poor performance of the Pakistan Army during wars, intensified the sense of insecurity in Pakistan. Moreover, the inconsistent arms supply and unreliable arms suppliers also became catalysts, in shaping Pakistan's threat perception.

## Modernisation of the Pakistan Army

Military modernisation largely depends on the country's financial strength and the ability to make strategic alliances. Lack of arms industry and financial constraints, forced Pakistan to make security and strategic alliance with the US/West. From the very beginning, Pakistan looked towards the US and the West, for obtaining arms. Pakistan signed security and defence pacts with the US and the West, in the 1950s, to procure arms and ammunitions. Particularly, Pakistan's security and defence pacts with the US, helped in procuring weapons, thus facilitating the modernisation of the Army. The Pakistan-US defence pact in May 1954, Pakistan's accession to the South East Asia Treaty Organisation (SEATO) later that year and joining the Baghdad Pact (later the Central Treaty Organisation, CENTO) in February 1955, were the events that changed the direction of the Pakistan Army.[7] Gen Ayub as the Army Chief, Defence Minister, and the President contributed in making strategic alliance with the US/West. With coming into the US/West alliance, the Pakistan Army received arms and funds from the US and the West. Gen Ayub initiated the modernisation process that was continued by the successive regimes.

Pakistan received arms, military and non-military aid from the US in the 1950s, but this was disrupted in the 1960s. The India-Pakistan War 1965 was the factor behind the discontinuity of the US arms supply to

---

[6] Stephen Philip Cohen, *The Idea of Pakistan* (Delhi: Oxford University Press, 2005), p. 104

[7] Brian Cloghley, *A History of the Pakistan Army: Wars and Insurrections* (Karachi: Oxford University Press, 2006), pp. 29-36

Pakistan. China's aggression on India in 1962, brought substantial changes in the attitude of the US towards the region in general, and India in particular. The US provided military and economic assistance to India in this period. India needed military and economic assistance to strengthen its military capability. In the event of the US and Britain arms supply embargo, Pakistan approached China and other countries for arms. China supplied arms to Pakistan during the 1965 war and continued that, even afterward.

In the 1970s, China supplied arms in bulk, to Pakistan. It supplied tanks that helped in building and reorganising the Pakistan Army. The US and other Western countries also supplied arms to Pakistan, in the 1970s, but these were in small quantity. Pakistan received military and economic assistance in bulk from the US/West, in the 1980s, because of the Soviet Union intervention in Afghanistan, in 1979. The US/West flow of arms and funds to Pakistan, helped in expanding and strengthening the Pakistan Army.

The Pakistan Army formed three new corps headquarters in the 1980s – XII Corps at Quetta (Baluchistan) in 1984-85, XXX Corps at Gujranwala (Punjab) 1986-87, and XXXI Corps Bahawalpur (Punjab) in 1986-87.

With the beginning of the Soviet withdrawal from Afghanistan in 1988, Pakistan's relevance to the US/West reduced. They discontinued their arms supply to Pakistan. As a result, the Pakistan Army faced challenges in procuring weapons. However, China had been consistently supplying arms to Pakistan. In the 1990s, Pakistan received arms, in bulk, from China that helped in boosting its arms modernisation programme. China was the only country that had been consistently supplying arms to Pakistan, since 1965. In the post-1965 and 1971 wars, China did not only supply T-59 tanks and the MIG fighter aircrafts, but also helped Pakistan in establishing the defence production industrial base at Pakistan Aeronautical Complex (PAC) Kamra, the Heavy Industries (HIT), and Heavy Mechanical and Electrical Complexes at Taxila.[8] Moreover, the defence complexes contributed to the modernisation of the Pakistan Army.

Even in the post-Zia period, the Army remained the centre of gravity and received resources for its development and modernisation. Pakistan

---

[8] Farooq Hameed Khan, "Towards an Everlasting Partnership", *The Nation*, 29 December, 2010

acquired missiles, systems, subsystems and missile related technology from various sources, among which China and North Korea are prominent. With induction of missiles, the combating capacity of the Pakistan Army, increased.

Pakistan's strategic significance for the US/West again increased in 2001, with the terrorist attacks in the US and Pakistan became an ally in the 'war against terror'. The US began to provide military and economic assistance to Pakistan to combat terrorism. The flow of the US weapons to Pakistan in the post-September 2001 was limited but was technologically advanced and sophisticated.

With 5,50,000 strength, modern and sophisticated arms, missiles, nuclear delivery capable missiles, and nuclear weapons, the Pakistan Army appears to be a modern Army. The striking capacity of the Pakistan Army has increased and the Army has divided the entire country into three offensive zones. The Pakistan Army has three offensive formations – Army Reserve North (ARN), Army Reserve South (ARS) and Army Reserve Central (ARC). The third formation Army Reserve Central (ARC) is in the raising process. Pakistan has a smaller forces and limited capability but will remain a significant player in the region.

## Arms Acquisitions and Defence Industry

Pakistan's arms acquisitions drive has immensely contributed in building its Armed Forces. The Pakistan Army received arms in bulk. Consequently, the Army has emerged as the most powerful entity in the country. With emergence as the most powerful institution in the country, the Army is involved in decision-making, particularly weapon acquisitions issues. The Army relatively, has the most power in matters pertaining to arms procurement and general defence decision-making.[9] The Army has been pursuing a policy to procure weapons from various sources.

Pakistan forged relations with the US/West in the 1950s to obtain arms and ensure its security. The US supplied arms to Pakistan besides giving economic assistance. Other Western European countries supplied

---

[9] Siddiqa-Agha, n. 1, p. 60

arms to Pakistan as well. In the 1960s, Pakistan tried to diversify the arms suppliers because of the imposition of the arms supply embargo by the US and Britain in 1965. As a result, the Eastern Bloc assumed significance in Pakistan's arms acquisition drive where China emerged as the major arms supplier. China supplied arms to Pakistan during the 1965 India-Pakistan War.

China had been consistently supplying arms to Pakistan, since the 1960s. Pakistan received tanks in bulk from China though these were of low quality. China also supplied other weapons to Pakistan that helped in strengthening the Army. Pakistan obtained arms in large quantities, from China, in the 1970s, that helped in expanding its defence industrial complex. China's arms supply to Pakistan got slow in the 1980s, due to some reasons, but was never disrupted. Pakistan continued to receive arms from China.

However, Pakistan continued its relation with the US and obtained arms from there too. The US and Britain supplied arms to Pakistan but these were expensive weapons. The US/West weapons were costly but sophisticated and advanced. Chinese weapons were not as sophisticated when compared to the US/West but were less expensive. Pakistan needed arms in huge quantity but cost and reliability were the main problems. Pakistan found China a reliable arms supplier and economically less expensive. In the 1970s, the US, Britain and other European countries supplied arms to Pakistan but these were in small quantities. The US/West supplied tanks, guns, Stinger missiles, and other sophisticated arms in large quantity to Pakistan, in the 1980s, because of the Soviet intervention in Afghanistan in 1979. But this did not continue in the 1990s. Pakistan and the US did not enjoy a warm relationship in the 1990s, as a result of which Pakistan received lesser arms from the US, during that time.

Pakistan's significance again increased for the US/West in 2001 with the terrorist attacks in the US. Pakistan became an ally in 'war against terror'. The US began to supply arms to Pakistan. China supplied arms to Pakistan, during this period, as well. The flow of arms from the US in the post-September 2001 was limited but was sophisticated and technologically-advanced.

Gen Ayub began to establish a defence production industry and this was continued by the successive regimes. Zulfiqar Ali Bhutto and Gen Zia established arms production industries. In the 1970s and 1980s, Pakistan established the weapons production factory with the Chinese help. Despite establishing ordnance factories, Pakistan could not produce its own weapons. Pakistan mainly modified and altered the designs and ranges of the weapons that were obtained from abroad.

## Composition of the Pakistan Army

The British recruitment policy changed after the 'Mutiny'of 1857 and the event was also called 'First-War of Independence'. With mutiny in 1857, the pattern of recruitment changed and brought greater number of Punjabis into armed forces.[10] After the 'Mutiny' of 1857, the British Government never ruled out the possibility of a similar uprising. It was only after the 1857 Mutiny that the British started to exclude certain groups from the colonial Army, on a systematic basis.[11] As a result, most of the recruitment was done from Punjab, NWFP, and Nepal, where political consciousness was dormant in comparison with other parts of India.[12] The people from Punjab region were willing to join the British Indian Army in return of the material benefits and greater employment opportunities. The British required ethnic groups that could not pose any challenge to sustaining its rule in India. As a result, the employment of the Punjabis increased from 32.7 percent in 1858 to 53.7 percent in 1910.[13] The ethnic composition in the Army was retained even after creation of Pakistan, and the British bias against recruitment of Bengalis, Baluch and Sindhis was maintained.

Nonetheless, the British Indian Army was represented by various sections and regions. At the time of partition, the strength of the British Indian Army was 11,800 officers and 450,000 other ranks.[14] During partition, Hindus, Sikhs and Muslims in the British Indian Army were free to choose

---

[10] Tan Tai Young, *The Garrison State* (Lahore: Vanguard, 2005), pp. 62-9

[11] Mustafa Kamal Pasha, *Colonial Political Economy* (Karachi: Oxford University Press, 1998), p. 135

[12] Hasan-Askari Rizvi, *The Military and Politics in Pakistan 1947-86* (Delhi: Konark Publishers, 1988), p. 18

[13] Young, n. 10, p. 71

[14] R S N Singh, *The Military Factor in Pakistan* (New Delhi: Lancer 2008), p. 350

between the Indian Armed Forces and the Pakistani Armed Forces. There were a few Muslims who opted to remain in the Indian Armed Forces while no Hindus/Sikhs personnel chose to stay in the Pakistani Armed Forces.[15] Muslims largely drew from Punjab. At the partition, there was not a single complete Muslim regiment that could come to Pakistan. After the First-War of Independence in 1857, the British changed the pattern of recruitment. They did not trust the Muslim soldiery to form independent all-Muslim units, though they needed them.[16] Therefore, Muslim soldiers remained scattered and mixed with others, to dilute their strength.

Of the Muslims recruited to the British Indian Army before the Second-World War, over 70 percent were from the Punjab province. The British Indian Army recruited manpower during the Second-World War, drew over 77 percent from Punjab, 19.5 percent from the NWFP, 2.2 percent from Sindh, and just 0.06 percent from Baluchistan.[17] Post-partition representation remained the same. After creation of Pakistan, Muslims of Punjab province dominated the Pakistan Army. The Punjabi Muslims' dominance in both the officer corps and other ranks remained.

There were no regular Bengali Muslim Army units during the Second-World War, although around sixty thousand Bengalis had been involved in construction units. The Pakistan Army had raised two battalions of the new East Bengal Regiment (EBR), partly from these units and partly from Muslims, who had served in the Bihar Regiment of the old British Indian Army.[18] The numbers of the EBR slowly increased. However, the Pakistan Army witnessed stiff resistance on the increasing representation of East Bengal, in the military.

From organisational perspective, these Bengali units were significant because they were the only single-class units in the new Pakistan Army. The EBR was a formidable force in the Pakistan Army. It had won more decorations for gallantry in the 1965 War than any other Pakistani Army

---

[15] Ibid.

[16] Hassan Abbas, *Pakistan's Drift into Extremism: Allah, the Army, and America's War on Terror* (New Delhi: Pentagon Press, 2005), p. 32

[17] Cohen, n. 5, p. 44

[18] Ibid, pp. 43-44

unit. Ansar, Mujahids and the Police, totalling 20000, constituted the hardcore of the fighters.[19] The Army had systematically accommodated different West Pakistani Muslims in different units, but not Bengalis. The discriminatory treatment against Bengali officers and people in other ranks, was also a major factor of armed resistance to the Pakistan Army, during the civil war in 1971. Despite Bengali agitation, the Pakistan Army did not take it seriously. Pakistan was running by the Army that the exclusion of Bengalis had broader political implications.

The present Pakistan Army is hardly more representative than the old one and a few districts of Punjab and NWFP are still as dominant as before. The bulk of the Army personnel come from the Punjab province. Around 75 percent of the Army is drawn from three districts of Punjab (Rawalpindi, Jhelum, and Campbellpur).[20] Another 20 percent are from three to four districts of the NWFP.[21] The other two provinces, Baluchistan and Sindh together represent only five percent in the Army.[22] The number of ethnic Baluch is less than the number of ethnic Sindhis in the Army. Pakistan's Air Force and Navy personnel are drawn from a much wider base. Pakistan military's recruitment pattern followed as the British pursued in recruiting military personnel from certain areas/regions. The continuation of earlier recruitment patterns, brought problems and brewed tension between the centre and provinces.

## Conclusion

The Pakistan Army has passed through various phases. With its inception in 1947, it began to expand its base and operational capacity. Pakistan made strategic alliance and signed defence pacts with the US and West to procure

---

[19] Lt-Gen B M Kaul, *Confrontation With Pakistan* (Delhi: Vikas Publications, 1971), p. 257

[20] Cohen, n. 5, p. 44; Stephen Philip Cohen, *The Idea of Pakistan* (Delhi: Oxford University Press, 2005), p. 224

[21] Ayesha Siddiqa, *Military Inc: Inside Pakistan's Military Economy* (London: Pluto Press, 2007), p. 59. Stephen P Cohen in his books *The Pakistan Army 1998 Edition,* and *The Idea of Pakistan* has explained the ethnic composition of the Pakistan Army. He has mentioned in his books that the only two districts (Kohat and Mardan) of NWFP represent 20 percent in the Army.

[22] Ibid

arms and strengthen its security. With induction of the US and West arms, the combating capacity of the Pakistan Army increased. But Pakistan could not maintain warm relationships with the US and West in the 1960s, as enjoyed by it in the 1950s. The event of the US and Britain arms supply embargo in 1965, on Pakistan, changed the military, particularly the Army. The 1971 military fiasco completely changed the Pakistan Army. Despite retaining power, the Pakistan Army could not avert dismemberment of East Pakistan.

China assumed a significant place in Pakistan's arms acquisitions policy in the 1970s. China began to supply arms to Pakistan, that contributed in nurturing the relationship between the two countries. The Chinese arms, particularly tanks, substantially contributed in strengthening the Pakistan Army. With the US, the West, and China's arms, the Pakistan Army was being expanded, developed and modernised. These arms tremendously contributed in enhancing the Pakistan Army's combating capacity and mobility. The Pakistan Army possesses modern and sophisticated weapons that are required for fighting. Pakistan has been facing challenges at its eastern and western borders. The Pakistan Army can not match with the Indian Army, in terms of numbers and otherwise. India has conventional superiority over Pakistan. The Pakistan Army has a small force and limited capacity, but will play a significant role in the region.

# 2

# Pakistan Army's Evolution and Development: 1947-71

Pakistan came into existence with India's partition in 1947. Pakistan initiated various measures to consolidate the newly created state. In the process of consolidation, Pakistan raised and expanded the Army, including Navy and Air Force. Pakistan got assets that were allotted to it, during the division. Gen Ayub Khan reorganised the Army and built an efficient fighting force. Pakistan's alliance with the West/US and security and defence pacts with them played a vital role in modernising and strengthening the Army. The US/West military and economic assistance helped in raising and expanding the Army. Moreover, China provided military and non-military assistance to Pakistan and helped in raising and developing the Pakistan Army. The Pakistan Army raised new units, divisions and organised corps headquarters.

The slow arms transfer to Pakistan led to rapid souring of relations between the two countries.[1] Immediately after the partition, India and Pakistan fought a war. After the First India-Pakistan War (1947-48), the Pakistan Army was reorganised, to enhance its combating capability. There was lack of balance between the fighting arms and the supporting services. Pakistan began to recruit personnel in order to strengthen the defence forces. The recruitment in the Army was urgently required because of three reasons. First, there was a shortage of manpower in the Army. Second, domestic disturbances and law and order problems required Army deployment. Third, the Army had to guard national frontiers/borders. From the military point of

---

[1] Brian Cloughley, *A History of the Pakistan Army: Wars and Insurrection* (Karachi: Oxford University Press, 1999), p. 4

view, Pakistan alone did not have the strategic depth or resources to withstand serious pressures from the northwest.

## Evolution of the Pakistan Army

Division of the British India Army between Pakistan and India had been planned before independence but actually took place few weeks before the partition. The Armed Forces Reconstitution Committee (AFRC) was constituted for the division of forces between the two dominions – India and Pakistan. After much debate, the AFRC had agreed to division of assets in the proportion of 64 percent to India and 36 percent to Pakistan. Pakistan received a fair share of personnel, but not enough to fill all vacancies. In the middle of chaos, the new Army had to grapple with the problems of creating balanced fighting forces. India received a high portion of base installations (stores and depots), because most of these were located within India itself.[2] Because of the disparity in size between India and Pakistan, the latter received fewer stores, supplies and facilities.[3] Pakistan received assets at the time of division, as was allotted.

Under the agreed formula for division of shared assets, Pakistan got 6 out of the 14 armoured regiments, 8 out of 40 artillery regiments, and 8 out of the 21 infantry regiments.[4] Of the infantry regiments comprising individual battalions, Pakistan received 33 and India got 88. The strength of the Pakistan Army reduced, as a result of which, several officers left for India. The reduced number of officers aggravated the Pakistan Army position. Many Army units with large numbers of Muslims, were in areas that were to remain in India; most of the defence-production facilities were situated in India, as were the bulk of military stores.[5] India retained those military stores which were situated in it.

There were 46 training establishments in pre-partition India, of which, 7 were located in Pakistan. These included the Staff College at Quetta, the

---

[2] Ibid., p. 3

[3] Stephen P Cohen, *The Pakistan Army 1998 Edition* (Karachi: Oxford University Press, 1998), p. 7

[4] Shuja Nawaz, *Crossed Swords: Pakistan, Its Army, and the Wars Within* (Karachi: Oxford University Press, 2008), p. 32; Stephen P Cohen, *The Pakistan Army 1998 Edition* (Karachi: Oxford University Press, 1998), p. 7

[5] Cohen, n. 3, p. 7

School of Military Intelligence and the Antiaircraft Artillery School, both at Karachi, the Royal Indian Army Service Corps (RIASC) School at Kakul, the No. 1 RIASC Training Centre (Supplies) at Lahore, the Armament Artificer Wing of the Indian Electrical and Mechanical Engineering Corps at Chklala (near Rawalpindi), and the Military Farms Department Training Centre at Lahore.

One of the key training centres that Pakistan got at partition was the Staff College at Quetta. It was closed down in September 1947 when the staff members left for India, but was re-opened in February 1948, under the British Brig J C A Lauder. Lt Col A M Yahya remained as instructor of the Staff College. Others joined Lt Col A M Yahya when the Staff College reopened. These officers were Lt. Col. Akhtar Hussain Malik and Lt Col Gul Nawaz Khan.

Though the Staff College was located in Pakistan, there were no major communications installations and other officer training establishments. The only technical school was at Nowshera in West Pakistan: the Army Service Corps School, was responsible for instruction in the management of supplies and transport.

The Pakistan Army had been facing logistics problems because of the shortage of the assets. The three main command workshops of the British Indian Army that helped in maintaining armoured fighting vehicles, radar repairs and crystal cutting remained in India, at Secunderabad, Kirkee, and Agra. Pakistan got five small retail depots out of the 40 ordnance depots, which were located in Pakistan. The major depots were located on the main supply routes which supported the Army during the war in South East Asia. The major stocks were kept in the major ports such as Bombay (Mumbai), Madras (Chennai), Calcutta (Kolkata), and supporting depots in Southern India. There were 12 engineering store depots in British India, of which three depots were located in Pakistan. Pakistan got three ordnance factories out of the 17 which were located there.

Pakistan started a new military headquarter in Rawalpindi, at the site of the headquarter of the British Indian Army's Northern Command from where the operations in the tribal areas were conducted. The General Headquarters (GHQ) in Pakistan was formed out of the Northern Command

Headquarters in Rawalpindi, with Gen Messervy as Commander-in-Chief (C-in-C) of the Pakistan Army. Initially, Pakistan faced shortage of officers, especially those with command experience. The Rawalpindi GHQ also headed six static area commands – Lahore, Rawalpindi, Peshawar, Waziristan, Sindh, and East Pakistan. The GHQ operated with few staff members, till October 1947, when most of its staff arrived from New Delhi, with their personal belonging and families, in many cases.

The Pakistan Army was facing severe constraint of human resources. At partition, the Pakistan Army was short of everything in the way of men, defence stores, weapons, ammunitions, and officers.[6] The immediate requirement for the planned Army of 1,50,000 men was around 4000 officers, of whom only 2500 were available.[7] The shortage of personnel in the combat units was around 50 percent. The shortage was filled with temporary commissions, short-service officers and the employment of 500 British officers. Hungarian and Polish officers were employed on contracts to run the medical corps, in order to fill the shortage. There were shortages of officers at technical places and in senior commanders. There were only one Pakistani major-general, two brigadiers, and 53 colonels.[8] There were only 100 Pakistani engineer officers and most of them, unqualified, were available for 600 appointments.[9] The gap was filled by the British, some of whom stayed on until the early 1950s. Initially, the Army existed only on the paper and gradually took shape.

In the beginning, command levels were firmly under British control. The C-in-C of the Pakistan Army was Gen Sir Frank Messervy, who was the chief of general staff (GOC) Northern Command in Rawalpindi at the time of independence, but he did not last long. Gen Sir Frank Messervy was succeeded by the COS Gen Sir Douglas Gracey, on 10 February 1948. The COS, the master general ordnance, and the quartermaster general

---

[6] Hassan Abbas, *Pakistan's Drift into Extremism: Allah, the Army, and America's War on Terror* (New Delhi: Pentagon Press, 2005), p. 32

[7] Cohen, n. 3, p. 7; R S N Singh, *The Military Factor in Pakistan* (New Delhi: Lancer 2008), p. 351

[8] Abbas, n. 6, p. 32; R S N Singh, *The Military Factor in Pakistan* (New Delhi: Lancer 2008), p. 351

[9] Cohen, n. 3, p. 7

were all British, as were the heads of the key directorates (signals, artillery, and military training) of the GHQ and even field formations. In building up and reorganisation of the Pakistan Army, the role of Gen Frank Messervy and Douglas Gracey cannot be disregarded.[10] Senior-level Pakistani officers were few and most of them did not even attain field rank, in pre-partition India. Some of these were quickly promoted, some beyond their experience and capacity, because of shortage of human resources. Early senior appointees were Brig Sher Khan, who headed the military operations directorate, and Col M Akbar Khan, who headed the weapons and equipment directorate.

Initially, the GHQ of the Pakistan Army was in the chaotic condition because of shortage of officers and command problem. New officers were coming every day from India and joining the Pakistan Army. There was the option for choice, as a result of which, some Muslim officers and jawans retained their position in the Indian Armed Forces. Navy and Air Force units and facilities that went to Pakistan were undermanned. There was a shortage of officers and even normal functions were affected. The chain of command was well defined on paper, but was hazy. The civilian leaders campaigned for independence under the flag of Muslim League and were busy in consolidating their position in the newly created state.

The Pakistan Army was organised into one armoured brigade, nine infantry brigades, and three artillery groups.[11] There were only nine regular officers in the Pakistan Navy and the Air Force had 65 pilots. Pakistan began to raise four divisions in West Pakistan and one division in East Pakistan in October 1947. Pakistan raised two cavalry units and four regiments between 1948 and 1950 that included the Bahawalpur Regiment (formerly Bahawalpure Princely State), Pathan Regiment (Frontier Force) recruited in the northwest, East Bengal Regiment (Bangladesh) and Azad Kashmir Regiment. The 7th Division was set up in Rawalpindi. The 8th Division was organised in Karachi/Quetta region and the 9th Division was formed for the NWFP. The Lahore area was reorganised as the 10th Division

[10] Abbas, n. 6, p. 32-33
[11] R S N Singh, *The Military Factor in Pakistan* (New Delhi: Lancer 2008), p. 351

and the 14th Division, in East Pakistan with the 3rd Armoured Brigade, at Risalpur.

The Pakistan Defence Council at its second meeting on October 2-3, 1947 agreed to establish the Pakistan Military Academy (PMA) at Kakul, which was to start operations in January 1948. The first commandant of the PMA was Col F H B Ingall of the 6th Lancers. Col F H B Ingall's main deputies were Lt Col M A Latif, as battalion commander and Lt Col Atiqur Rehman, as chief instructor. The first trainees were from the group of officer cadets, from the Indian Military Academy (IMA) in Dehra Dun, who went to Lahore in October 1947. The group comprised of the second and third IMA courses. The members of the second course were commissioned in the Pakistan Army. The members of the third course were remained temporarily, with units and later joined the PMA, when it started functioning out of the former Army Service Corps School premises.

Developments during the partition and after, brought about stress in the process of consolidating the newly formed state. The India-Pakistan War 1947-48 created economic problem for Pakistan, consequently economic stress brought constraints in raising the Armed Forces. Pakistan had not yet expanded its relation with other countries and had a few friends. "Despite the Army's preoccupation with events following partition, it had succeeded in building itself a fairly firm foundation by the beginning of 1951."[12] The Pakistan Army had taken a firm and definite shape by 1951 and began to expand.

## Emerging Role of Pakistan Army

The Pakistan Defence Council, in its first meeting on 5-6 September 1947, outlined aims and objectives of the Army. It was headed by the Prime Minister and Defence Minister Liaqat Ali Khan. The meeting outlined the internal and external functions of the Army. The functions of the Army were to assist the civil government in maintaining law and order, and to support the political authorities in the tribal region. The Army had relatively small resources. The lack of resources constrained the Army's functions and the

---

[12] Fazal Muqeem Khan, *The History of The Pakistan Army* (Karachi: Oxford University Press, 1963), p. 137

external role was defined in the British imperial defence terms, to prevent aggression by a minor power while preparing to defend against a major power.[13] The Army had to perform huge task because physical boundary made its border difficult to defend. Pakistan shared long borders with India and around 1350 miles with Afghanistan. The Iranian border did not figure at that time in Pakistan's strategy of border defence.

Law and order problem, Ahmedia riots in the early 1950s, political instability, dwindling influence of the Muslim League and finally its disintegration, created a fragile political atmosphere in Pakistan. The role of the Army expanded as its involvement grew. As a result, Pakistan Army's influence increased. The Army was expanded and raised new units to increase its combating capability.

## Defence Expenditure 1947-58

Pakistan allocated substantial resources for its defence preparedness despite financial constrains. The Pakistan Army received a large chunk of its total defence budget. Below, Table 1 demonstrates that defence expenditure was high, despite financial problems. Defence expenditure was more than 50 percent of its total government expenditure. Despite economic problems and financial constraints, Pakistan allocated huge resources to its military. Pakistan's defence expenditure never came down below 50 percent of its total government expenditure in the period of 1947-58, as Table 1 shows.

---

[13] Nawaz, n. 4, p. 34

**Defence Expenditure 1947-58**

| Year (April to March) | In Million Rupees | Percentage of the total Government Expenditure |
|:---:|:---:|:---:|
| 1947-48 | 236.0 | 65.16 |
| 1948-49 | 461.5 | 71.32 |
| 1949-50 | 625.4 | 73.6 |
| 1950-51 | 649.9 | 51.32 |
| 1951-52 | 792.4 | 54.94 |
| 1952-53 | 725.7 | 56.68 |
| 1953-54 | 633.2 | 58.7 |
| 1954-55 | 640.5 | 57.5 |
| 1955-56 | 917.7 | 64.0 |
| 1956-57 | 800.9 | 60.1 |
| 1957-58 | 854.2 | 56.1 |

Source: Hasan Askari Rizvi, *The Military and Politics in Pakistan 1947-86* (Delhi: Konark Publishers, 1988), pp. 43-44

**Table: 1**

Pakistan kept the defence expenditure high, in order to bolster its security. The huge defence budget enabled expansion of the Pakistan Army. Modern arms were procured and inducted into the Pakistan Army, to increase fighting capability. The government made attempts in the years of 1947-48 to curtail expenditure of the Army and to disband the Armoured Brigade that the Pakistan Army possessed, because the Army could not afford such expensive equipment and maintain it satisfactorily.[14] But the government could not curtail expenditure of the Army, due to stiff resistance, within the establishment.

[14] Mazhar Aziz, *The Military Control in Pakistan: The Parallel State* (New York: Routledge, 2008), p. 60He reorganised the Frontier units and enlarged the Baluch Regiment. The Baluch Regiment was expanded by absorbing 8 Punjab and the Bahawalpur Regiment. The Frontier Force Regiment absorbed the FF Rifles and the Pathan Regiment; and 1, 14, 15, and 16 Punjabis formed the Punjab Regiment. The reorganisation in the Army again took place in 1956. Gen Ayub's efforts yielded fruits and the Army was expanded.

Developments at the time of partition and the aftermath, generated a sense of insecurity in Pakistan. Security concerns compelled the establishment to allocate huge resources for filling the gaps. Civilian leaders kept defence budgets high, in order to expand and strengthen the military. Although Prime Minister Bogra (East Pakistani) had tried to introduce a bill to cut the size of the Armed Forces, he reversed it due to stiff resistance in Pakistan.

## Ayub and the Army

Gen Ayub Khan replaced Gen Gracey as C-in-C, on 17 January 1951 and got three extensions, as C-in-C of the new Army. The growth of the Pakistan Army in the 1950s and 1960s was attributed to Ayub Khan, as the Army Chief, Defence Minister, and President. The Ayub period can be attributed to the expansion of the Army and improvement in training and administration, a military coup, Pakistan's involvement with Baghdad Pact/CENTO and SEATO, diminution of British influence, expansion of the US ties, particularly regarding acquisition of defence weapons and equipments, expansion of Pakistan-China ties, tensions with India, political uncertainty, and growth of corruption.

Gen Ayub took personal interest in improving the Army and initiated various measures to achieve it. He carried out reforms which he gradually implemented. He prescribed an Army training cycle, and set objectives to be met by every unit and formation. He visited throughout the country to see the Army, particularly while units were conducting exercises. In Gen Ayub's view, the Army had to modernise itself, in every aspect. He stressed and concentrated on the training of the officers. He viewed that the Army training centres should not get involved in training of non-combat tradesmen such as clerks, drivers, cooks since it was not cost-effective.He thought that each trade should have a central school of training which should be introduced quickly.

The Army built schools, gun sheds, tank parks, rifle ranges, accommodation, and instructional centres. The schools of artillery and armour were established at Nowshera on the Grand Trunk Road, about thirty miles west of Rawalpindi, where the GHQ was being expanded. The Engineering School was established at Risalpur, about five miles north of Rawalpindi.

The Pakistan Military Academy (PMA) for training of officers was built at Kakul near Abbottabad, about fifty miles north of Rawalpindi. Other schools and training centres were established one after another in the following years. The Staff College, at Quetta in Baluchistan, that opened in 1905, produced many distinguished officers and was expanded in the Ayub period.

The British Training Advisory Staff had been withdrawn at the end of the agreed time. In Ayub's view, the discontinuity of the foreign training staff was needed because they would not meet the requirements of Pakistan. For Ayub and his staff officers, the organisation had become invaluable. Gen Musa created the Directorate of Military Training (DMT) since it was inappropriate that the Army had to rely on foreigners, for its training expertise. But the gap was felt and took a long time to fill.

appointed Gen Mohammad Musa Khan as the C-in-C of the Pakistan Army, on 28 October, 1958. Gen Musa abolished the post of the Chief of Staff (COS), one of the most important appointments in a senior commander's headquarters. It was a major change in the Army since the COS acted as a high-powered appointment in the Army. Gen Musa remained as the C-in-C, till September 1966.

There was constant pressure to create more corps HQ to manage various formations. Arguments in support of creation of more corps HQ were put forward but failed to get high-level support. There were two responsible factors that became obstacles in the creation of the corps HQ: financial constrains and lack of efficient officers. After the 1965 war, the Army was organised into 2 Corps Headquarters, 8 Infantry Divisions and 1 Armoured Division.[15] The 1965 war highlighted the shortcomings of the Pakistan Army – organisational, training, and arms.

## Joining the Western Alliance

Gen Ayub went Washington with the prime minister and foreign minister in October 1953. After their visit to the US, President Ghulam Mohammad went there in November 1953. The high dignitary visits to the US was a reflection of the growing close relation between the two countries. Pakistan

---

[15] Singh, n. 11, p. 356

nurtured relations with the US, that yielded tangible results in the years to come. Pakistan received military and non-military aid from the US in the 1950s and onwards. The Pakistan Army obtained arms from the US that helped in its expansion. The fear of India's domination became a very important factor in Pakistan's internal politics and foreign relations.[16] As a result, Pakistan continued to grapple with a sense of insecurity.

Pakistan and the US signed a Mutual Defence Assistance Agreement in May 1954. For the US, signing such an agreement meant expansion of its presence, in the region. For Pakistan, the agreement provided modern arms and equipments, that required it. In association with the US, Pakistan Army (Air Force and Navy) began to enjoy many benefits. The Army created an armoured division of two brigades and an independent armoured brigade. Pakistan received enough materials to equip seven infantry divisions. The Pakistan Air Force also received equipments and airfields and was improved with the induction of the new F-86 Sabre aircraft. The Pakistan Navy also got assistance and the ports of Chittagong and Karachi were modernised. Pakistani officers went to the US for training and there were regular exercises with other countries' forces including Iran, Britain and Turkey.

The introduction of the Mutual Defence Assistance Agreement in May 1954, accession to the South East Asia Treaty Organisation (SEATO) later that year, and joining the Baghdad Pact (later the Central Treaty Organisation, CENTO) in February 1955, were some of the key events that had critical impacts on "the direction of the Pakistan Army – and of Pakistan".[17] Pakistan's association with these organisations, facilitated acquisition of arms for the Army.

The US was a member of the SEATO and had a considerable leverage over its members but was not a member of the Baghdad Pact/CENTO (although it had a considerable influence on the group). The US considered both organisations to be bastions against the Soviet Union. However, Pakistan

---

[16] Hasan-Askari Rizvi, *The Military and Politics in Pakistan 1947-86* (Delhi: Konark Publishers, 1988), p. 39

[17] Cloughley, n. 1, p. 31

thought otherwise and the Soviet Union was not on its high priority of security threats. Pakistan considered India as a 'primary threat'. With the joining of the Baghdad Pact/CENTO, SEATO and signing a military assistance agreement with the US, it appeared to Pakistan that it had a security guarantee in case of any event of conflict with India. It was a mistake on the part of Pakistan. The US had opposite views and sought to contain the Soviet expansion. The US and Pakistan's divergent views laid the foundation for 'irritation' and 'flounder' in the US-Pakistan relationship.

Pakistan and the US signed another agreement in March 1955 that had international ramifications. 'The Pakistan-US Communications Unit Agreement' was signed on 5 March 1955, that provided the US 'for the establishment and operation of a communications unit at Peshawar, certain military rights and facilities and a status of forces agreement'. The 'certain military rights' comprised of the use of the Peshawar airfield by U-2 aircraft, to overfly the Soviet Union, illegally. The Soviet Union warned Pakistan for 'severe consequences'.

In March 1959, the Pakistan-US Bilateral Agreement of Cooperation was signed, and the US agreed to provide military aid to Pakistan.[18] The US aid, through offset purchases, soft loans, direct grants, and training assistance, had considerably helped in modernising the Army, including Navy and Air Force. "The Army grew more confident and proficient as new equipment arrived and training doctrine evolved."[19] Schools of instruction expanded and modernised. As a result, standards improved. Pakistan's armour, artillery and infantry substantially improved with the US connection. The armour, artillery and other technical services and branches were strongly influenced by the US practices.[20] In only artillery, more than 200 Pakistani officers went for training in the US, between 1955 and 1958. The US approach entered into solving problems, along with the American weapons and training. The US connection led to revision in the organisational structure of the Pakistan Army.

---

[18] General Khalid Mahmud Arif, *Working with Zia: Pakistan's Power Politics 1977-1988* (Karachi: Oxford University Press, 1995), p. 331

[19] Cloughley, n. 1, p. 34

[20] Stephen Philip Cohen, *The Idea of Pakistan* (Delhi: Oxford University Press, 2005), p. 102

Pakistan had defence problems on its western border – Afghanistan. The government of Afghanistan strongly opposed the demarcation of the border – the Durand Line. The Afghan border was disturbed (the region had never been quiet), and the tribes in the region, created problems. Khrushchev and Bulganin visited Kabul in December 1955, where they declared that they sympathised with Afghanistan's policy on the Pakhtunistan issue. The Soviet Union gave US $300 million in aid to Afghanistan in the next five years, including that used in construction of military airfields and other military assistance. The development alarmed the US. The Soviet involvement in Afghanistan brought closer US-Pakistan military cooperation.

## The 1965 War and its Impact

High defence expenditure, the Pakistan-US defence agreements, and Pakistan's alliance with the US/West did not yield results during the 1965 war, as expected and Pakistan failed to withstand the Indian pressure. India had performed well during the war and Pakistan was forced to declare ceasefire on 22 September 1965. Militarily, Pakistan came under pressure. Politically, the post-1965 war period witnessed the decline of Ayub and the rise of Zulfiqar Ali Bhutto. Pakistan felt the limitations of the US/West alliance.

China's aggression on India in 1962 had emboldened Pakistan. Pakistan could not adequately assess the strength of the Indian Army's capabilities and crossed the LoC in Kashmir, in August 1965. The GHQ in Rawalpindi conducted its annual assessments of the Indian Army's capabilities, in 1963 and 1964 and drew the conclusion that the Indian Army had changed little since the India-China War of 1962. It was a completely inadequate assessment about the Indian Army. Pakistan overestimated its Army's capabilities and entered into Indian territories. India retaliated and Pakistan had no option except to declare cease-fire on 22 September, 1965. Pakistan paid the price for its poor assessment of the Indian Army.

The UN Secretary General, U Thant visited India and Pakistan from 9-11 September 1965, to persuade their leaders for ceasefire. But he failed to persuade the leaders of either country to declare an unconditional ceasefire. He went first to Pakistan, and then to India. Ayub insisted that an agreement for a ceasefire must include an arrangement for settlement of the Kashmir dispute. Negotiations continued in New York, as the Soviets, Americans, British and French were apprehensive about China entering the war. China sent a belligerent statement on 16 September 1965, indicating support for Pakistan. Ayub and Bhutto paid a visit to China on 20/21 September 1965 and met Chinese Prime Minister and Defence Minister. Pakistan received China's support but it was below expectation.[21] India had an edge over Pakistan in many ways.

The US imposed arms embargo on both warring countries, Pakistan and India. Pakistan relied almost entirely on the US and Britain for arms and ammunitions. Pakistan came under pressure because of shortage of arms and ammunitions and the US arms embargo. The US and Britain embargo on supply of arms to Pakistan, had adverse effects on its defence forces. Pakistan had defence agreement with the US. Under the Pakistan-US 1959 agreement, the US would have to 'assist the Government of Pakistan at its request' if there were a threat to its 'national independence and integrity'. Pakistan was heavily outnumbered, short of arms and ammunitions, and subject to increasing international pressure. Despite the US commitment to Pakistan under the SEATO, CENTO, and the bilateral defence agreement of 1959, the US imposed arms supply embargo on it during the 1965 war. The US attitude towards Pakistan and the Arms supply embargo during the 1965 War shook up not only Pakistan but also had badly shaken the Shah of Iran, who signed an Arms deal with the Soviet Union in 1967.[22] The US action had an impact, not only on Pakistan but also on Iran and other countries.

Finally, Ayub announced ceasefire on 22 September 1965 and the war came to an end on 23 September. The shortage of arms and the US Arms embargo on Pakistan, forced Ayub to announce ceasefire on 22 September 1965.[23] Ayub had no option but to declare ceasefire. The Pakistan Army had faced problems due to shortage of arms and ammunitions. Pakistan learnt lesson about the limits of the external alliances.

---

[21] Cloughley, n. 1, p. 100

[22] Prithvi Ram Mudiam, *India and the Middle East* (London: British Academic Press, 1994), pp 74-77

[23] Ian Talbot, *Pakistan, A Modern History* (London: Hurst & Company, 2005), pp. 175-78

The 1965 War had adverse impact over Pakistan in general and the Ayub rule in particular. On the one hand, the 1965 War seriously damaged Ayub's image and declined his popularity. On the other hand, Zulfiqar Ali Bhutto's popularity was soaring. The decline of Ayub and rise of Bhutto was the product of the 1965 War. Pakistan's economy and Armed Forces had been adversely affected. On the other hand, Pakistan's relation with the US was seriously affected, while China and the Eastern Bloc began to assume greater importance in diplomacy and as suppliers of military equipment.

China supplied arms to Pakistan during the 1965 War. China's attitude towards the region in general and Pakistan in particular, changed as a result of the India-China War 1962 and the changing attitude of the US towards the region, particularly India. China's aggression over India in 1962 and India's comprehensive defeat changed the US attitude towards India and the surrounding region. India's relation with the US and Britain became extensive and energetic after the China-India War 1962. The US and Britain supplied arms to India. The US and Britain arms supply policy was intended to strengthen India's military capacity that could counter China. India required the US/West military and non-military aid to meet security challenges. The growing US-India relation, the US arms supply to India, the India-Pakistan War of 1965 and the US attitude towards the 1965 War played a vital role in shaping China's arms transfer policy towards Pakistan. China's belief in continuing arms supply to Pakistan, further strengthened with the India-Pakistan War 1971 and the dismemberment of East Pakistan. The 1971 event added complexity in the region. China believed that consistent arms supply to Pakistan was needed. The 1965 and 1971 wars brought perceptible changes in China's attitude towards Pakistan and pursued policies to strengthen Pakistan, militarily. As a result, China supplied tanks and other weapons in bulk, to Pakistan. The Pakistan Army received tanks and other arms that strengthened its combating capacity.

Gen Musa Khan retired from the post of the C-in-C in September 1966. After retiring as C-in-C, Gen Musa Khan became Governor of East Pakistan. East Pakistan needed a person who would have sympathy for the Bengalis and counter the Punjabis officials, politicians, and military officers, who considered the East, a poor and backward adjunct to West Pakistan. East Pakistan was the largest contributor to the Pakistani economy but West Pakistan did not allocate adequate resources for alleviation of poverty in East Pakistan and its economic development.

### Defence Expenditure 1958-71

| Year (April to March) | In Million Rupees | Percentage of the Total Government Expenditure |
|:---:|:---:|:---:|
| 1958-59 | 996.6 | 50.9 |
| 1959-60 | 1043.5 | 56.51 |
| 1960-61 | 1112.4 | 58.73 |
| 1961-62 | 1108.6 | 55.80 |
| 1962-63 | 954.3 | 53.16 |
| 1963-64 | 1156.5 | 49.49 |
| 1964-65 | 1262.3 | 46.07 |
| 1965-66 | 2855.0 | 53.67 |
| 1966-67 | 2293.5 | 60.92 |
| 1967-68 | 2186.5 | 53.63 |
| 1968-69 | 2426.8 | 55.62 |
| 1969-70 | 2749.1 | 53.35 |
| 1970-71 | 3201.5 | 55.66 |

Source: Hasan-Askari Rizvi, *The Military and Politics in Pakistan 1947-86* (Delhi Konark Publishers, 1988), pp. 124-25

### Table: 2

Table 2 shows defence expenditure from 1958 to 1971. Pakistan allocated huge resources for defence and a large portion was received by the Pakistan Army. But performance of the Pakistan Army, during the 1965 War, was poor. Pakistan was defeated in the 1971 War with India and East Pakistan, dismembered permanently. The poor performance of the Pakistan Army during the 1971 War, resulted in dismemberment of East Pakistan. The 1971 debacle brought perceptible changes in the Pakistan Army. In the post-1971 scenario, the Pakistan Army was reorganised.

## The Army and the 1965 War

The US military assistance to Pakistan, from 1953 onwards, helped in strengthening its Armed Forces. By 1959, Pakistan had become much stronger because of acquisitions of the US/Western weapons. The balance between the armed might of India and Pakistan, began to tilt more in favour of Pakistan, at least in quality, with the substantial aid received from the US, in the shape of sophisticated tanks, artillery, aircrafts, and radar equipment.[24] Pakistan enjoyed a warm relationship with the US in the 1950s. As a result, it received military and economic aid from the US/West.

In 1965, the Indian Army was about 800000, consisting of 16 divisions of full strength (nine of which were mountain formations), and had about 1000 armoured fighting vehicles, including reserves, and about 2500 pieces of artillery.[25] By 1965, the Pakistan Army had also improved, with induction of the US/Western weapons. In 1965, the strength of the Pakistan Army was about 250000 and it had eight divisions; in addition there were a large number of Mujahids, Razakars and other irregulars.[26] Pakistan had around 800 armoured fighting vehicles, including modern Pattons. Its artillery was less impressive in comparison to that of India but it had better guns.[27] Pakistan possessed the US/Western weapons and equipments but could not withstand Indian pressure and counter-attacks.

There were inadequate weapons, insufficient ammunition, and lack of the US support. The 1965 War exposed that there had been inadequate training at all unit levels, misguided selection of officers for some higher

---

[24] Lt Gen B. M. Kaul, *Confrontation With Pakistan* (Delhi: Vikas Publications, 1971), p. 17
[25] Ibid.
[26] Ibid.
[27] Ibid., p. 18

command appointments, poor command and control arrangements, poor intelligence gathering and bad intelligence procedures. In spite of shortcomings, the Pakistan Army had managed to fight the large Indian Army. The Pakistan Air Force had fought well in countering the much larger Indian Air Force and supported the ground forces. The Pakistan Air Force was well handled and controlled by the Commander-in-Chief, Nur Khan. There was good cooperation between the Army and Air Force, at all levels, during the war. The Pakistan Army had been facing some serious challenges, since ill-trained and inefficient officers occupied the higher positions.

The Pakistan Army had been suffering from appointment and promotions problems that became acute in later years. The appointment of senior commanders and staff officers was made on grounds of loyalty to Presidents. In spite of many difficulties, headquarters and units were able to maintain communication much of the time. However, good signal training at the individual level and effective use of line, required procurement of modern radios and good communications. On both sides, (Pakistan and India) communications security was poor, particularly at the officer level. Codes were compromised and broken, and individual identities, unit identification and locations were detected.

The 1965 War had thrown light on the shortcomings of the Pakistan Army. However, the Pakistan Army made efforts to improve its force structure, administration, equipment, training, and every aspect of military potentiality. In the aftermath of the India-Pakistan War 1965, the Pakistan Army brought in organisational and technical changes. Till 1965, the Army was based on divisions which were operationally controlled, directly, by the GHQ. The Pakistan Army had only one Corps Headquarters. After retirement of Gen Musa Khan as C-in-C in September 1966, the Army raised IV Corps at Lahore, in Punjab. Gen Yahya Khan succeeded Gen Musa Khan as C-in-C. Actually, it was Yahya Khan who initiated some major changes in the Pakistan Army.

Pakistan began to strengthen its Armed Forces in the post-1965 War, since it had only one corps. The Pakistan Army was considerably strengthened with procuring weapons, raising units and recruiting manpower.

By 1967, the strength of the Army increased to 300000, including 25000 Azad Kashmir troops.[28] It had three armoured divisions and some independent armoured units, with 1400 tanks and about 450 combat aircrafts; two new divisions had been raised, 17 in place of 9 and 33 in place of 16.[29] This provided Pakistan, 14 infantry and 3 armoured divisions. It increased to double Pakistan's striking capability, since 1965.

Nonetheless, the Pakistan Army had been facing problems at the organisation and leadership levels in the late 1960s. The GHQ had been as ineffective before the outbreak of the 1971 War, as never before. The performance of the Pakistan Army was poor during the India-Pakistan War of 1971. As a result, East Pakistan permanently broke away. The Bengali resentment was against both the military and West Pakistan. The Army in East Pakistan was not sufficiently and adequately equipped. West Pakistan denied expansion and modernisation of the military in East Pakistan. The 1971 War reflects a complete failure of the Pakistani military leadership, particularly the Army.

**Diversifying Arms Suppliers**

Pakistan had to rely on foreign arms suppliers because of lack of defence production industry in the country. There were several ordnance factories at the time of partition but only three were located in Pakistan. The Pakistan Ordnance Factory at Wah, near Rawalpindi, was new and capable of manufacturing only minor items. Pakistan bought weapons from the US/West. The US supplied weapons to Pakistan as a part of military assistance programmes. But the US and Britain arms supply to Pakistan was disrupted in 1965 because of the India-Pakistan War. Pakistan sought arms and ammunitions during the war, but time was too short for arms to arrive in huge quantities. There were no alternatives available with the US and Britain for resupply of arms and ammunitions since both had imposed arms embargo.

The disruption of arms supply created problems for Pakistan since it was dependent on their arms. Islamabad felt betrayed by Washington because despite their alliance relationship, the US not only refused to help Pakistan

---

[28] *The Military Balance 1967-68*, p. 32
[29] Kaul, n. 24, p. 244

during the 1965 War, but it also imposed an arms embargo on both the warring states.[30] The US attitude towards the India-Pakistan War, 1965 and its arms supply embargo had shaken Pakistan. "The US arms embargo to both India and Pakistan worked out to India's advantage, because India was almost self-sufficient in small arms and ammunition production, whereas Pakistan was excessively dependent on the West for the same."[31] The Arms embargo had severely affected Pakistan but India sailed through because it possessed vast reserves. Being disillusioned with the US, Pakistan cultivated and nourished a closer relationship with China.[32] Beijing started to supply arms to Pakistan, that strengthened its Army.

For Pakistan, it was essential to engage in more reliable suppliers and to diversify sources. But diversification had its own problems. Acquisition of a number of different systems from different sources could impose strains on availability of spare parts, logistics, technical support from base workshops to battlefield, training (technical and operational), and interoperability. Apparently, it was better to stick to one supplier for an item like tanks and ensure that spares could be manufactured or obtained, in open market, rather than having different types of tanks, each requiring different means of support. This argument supported dependency on a particular source for weapons acquisitions, that was undesirable for Pakistan. This approach was not followed by Pakistan and Pakistan sought alternate sources for weapons acquisitions.

Reliance on foreign suppliers for arms and ammunitions was a more complex issue than simply identifying what was needed. For Pakistan, the main points were quality, cost, and guarantee of supply. The US and Britain produced most of the best systems, but had proved to be unreliable suppliers. China's aggression over India in 1962 compelled the US to think over India's security. The US provided military aid to India after the 1962 War.[33] The US and Britain military aid to India in the period 1962-65 had been energetic and extensive. Pakistan regarded supply of arms to India, as a threat to its existence. Pakistan considered that weapons supplied by the US and Britain

---

[30] Bhumitra Chakma, *Pakistan's Nuclear Weapons* (London: Routledge, 2009), p. 16

[31] Mudiam, n. 22, p. 75

[32] Chakma, n. 30, p. 16

[33] Arif, n. 18, p. 331

to India, were not intended to counter China but were intended to use against their ally (Pakistan). As a result, Pakistan was wary of western powers.[34] The US and Britain arms supply to India, after India's debacle in the 1962 War, intended to counter China's growing prowess.

President Ayub went to the US in December 1965, to talk with President Johnson. President Johnson made it clear that the US relation with Pakistan was over. Pakistan "developed friendly ties with China, a step that was highly distasteful to the US"[35]. The growing ties between Pakistan and China, were resented by the US. Pakistan was not prepared to give up its relationship with China, since it could provide meaningful assistance to Pakistan – political, security, diplomatic, arms and ammunitions, and economic. It could be a reliable strategic ally. It was China which openly supported Pakistan, during the 1965 War. Turkey, Iran, Indonesia, Jordan and Saudi Arabia supported Pakistan, during the 1965 War, but none of these countries had a modern arms industry, and all had problems. With the US arms supply embargo, Pakistan began to tap other sources like Germany, France, Italy and the Soviet Union for defence procurement.[36] Pakistan began to expand its relations with other countries in order to procure arms from them.

The Soviet Union also provided economic and military assistance to Pakistan in 1966, which annoyed India and did not please the US. The Soviet Union supplied weapons to Pakistan - 100 T-54/T-55 tanks, around 200 130mm guns and vehicles in 1968 and 1969.[37] Pakistan received Mi-8 helicopters from the Soviet Union in 1970-71.[38] Prime Minister Indira Gandhi complained to the Soviet Union, concerning the supply of arms to Pakistan. After India's objection, the Soviet Union downgraded its relations with Pakistan.

China supplied arms to Pakistan during the 1965 war and after. China's President Liu Shao-chi and Foreign Minister Chen Yi visited Pakistan in

---

[34] Cloughley, n. 1, p. 118-19

[35] Arif, n. 18, p. 331

[36] Singh, n. 11, p. 358

[37] *The Military Balance 1968-69*; and *SIPRI Yearbook 1969-70*, p. 348

[38] *SIPRI Yearbook 1972*, p. 136

March 1966. Before the Chinese President's visit, for the first time, tanks and aircrafts appeared officially at the National Day Parade, on 23 March 1966. Vehicles, small arms and ancillary items to equip three infantry divisions, were also supplied by China.

The US and Britain thought of resumption of arms supply to Pakistan in 1966, in the light of Chinese guarantees and the Soviet overtures. The US restarted economic aid programmes to India and Pakistan in June 1966, and gradually extended it to include supply of defence equipments, but the US and the West had by then lost what could have been their constant friends - not just in Pakistan but elsewhere.[39] While the US began military assistance to Pakistan in June 1966, it appeared to China that Pakistan was tilting towards the US. China's Prime Minister Zhou Enlai paid a visit to Pakistan, in July 1966, where Ayub assured him that the Pakistan-China friendship would continue to flourish. The most significant outcome of the 1965 War was that Pakistan increasingly became dependent on China, for its defence needs.[40] The Pakistan Army raised three infantry divisions, with Chinese help immediately after the India-Pakistan War, 1965. These divisions were equipped with Chinese arms. China supplied around 900 tanks and other equipments. Pakistan needed arms while China was equally interested in making a strategic partnership with Pakistan and expansion of its presence, in the region.

Pakistan acquired T-54, T-55, and T-59 Chinese tanks in 1970, to improve its firepower capability and also received 300 armoured personnel carriers (APCs) from the US.[41] Pakistan was convinced that the armoured operations against India had failed in the Punjab theatre, during the 1965 War because the infantry which had to follow up the armour had failed to do so as it lacked armoured personnel carriers to transport it over the bullet-swept areas in battle.[42] As a result, Pakistan sought the APCs from the US.

---

[39] Cloughley, n. 1, p. 122
[40] Singh, n. 11, p. 357
[41] *The Military Balance, 1969-70 and 1970-71.*
[42] Kaul, n. 24, p. 115

The US military mission visited Pakistan in July 1967. The US allowed Pakistan to purchase spares for the inventory of the American weapons. This comprised F-104 fighters, B-57 light bombers, and M-113 armoured personnel carriers. In fact, the US had supplied little amount of weapons in the last five years. Gen Yahya had established contact with Richard Nixon, who became the US President in 1969. Nixon had already visited Pakistan in 1953, when he was Eisenhower's Vice-President. President Nixon preferred anyone to Indira Gandhi. Nixon was anti-India and pro-Pakistan.[43] President Nixon had sought diplomatic success where Gen Yahya was to play an important part in rapprochement between the US and China. By the late 1960s, alignment in the region began to take shape. Pakistan played a key role in arranging meetings between China and the US and normalising the relation between them. However, Pakistan fell in serious crisis in the early 1970s and East Pakistan was dismembered permanently.

## Conclusion

Pakistan had been facing serious challenges in raising its Army in the early days of its inception. The newly created state did not have sufficient resources to meet the requirements of raising units and divisions. Lack of manpower, unreliable arms suppliers, and financial constraints were major challenges that the Army had been facing. Gen Ayub as the Army chief, Army Chief-cum-Defence Minister, and finally President, was keen on improving the Army. He allocated resources to expand and improve the Army. Gen Ayub made efforts for the expansion of the Army and he significantly contributed to its development. In the Ayub period, the Army was reorganised and expanded.

Pakistan's strategy of alignment with foreign powers in the 1950s, paid dividends and helped in expanding the Army. Pakistan signed defence and security pacts with the US, in the 1950s. Such pacts facilitated the flow of the US/West military and economic aid to Pakistan that contributed in expansion of the Army. The flow of the US/West arms to Pakistan immensely contributed in strengthening the Army. As a result, the Pakistan Army's dependency on the US, grew. The performance of the Pakistan

---

[43] Cloughley, n. 1, p. 131

Army during the India-Pakistan War 1965, was poor, despite the US/West arms. The effects of Pakistan Army's heavy dependency over the US/West arms were witnessed, during the 1965 War. They were severe and devastating.

Pakistan approached other countries for arms, to curtail its dependency on the US and Britain. China supplied arms to Pakistan during the 1965 War and after. Russia also supplied arms to Pakistan but those were limited in quantity and for a short period. The Pakistan Army received the Chinese tanks that transformed its capability, though these were not of high quality. The Pakistan Army raised three infantry divisions with Chinese assistance, immediately after the 1965 war. By 1967, the Pakistan Army could form only two corps, despite the US/West and Chinese military and financial aid. The Pakistan Army required finance and military aid to increase its combating capacity. For the Pakistan Army, arms and training of officers were needed at every level.

# 3

# Post-1971 Modernisation of the Pakistan Army

Pakistan had been facing serious challenges in the early 1970s. The loss of East Pakistan in 1971 and serious problems in the residual Pakistan raised questions over the survival of the country. Zulfiqar Ali Bhutto assumed power while Pakistan was passing through the gravest crises. Bhutto initiated various measures to strengthen and modernise the Armed Forces. He restructured the military in general and the Army in particular. He allocated substantial resources to strengthen the Army. In the post-Bhutto period, the successive regimes in Pakistan, made efforts to modernise the Army. The Pakistan Army was organisationally strengthened and its size was increased. As a result, the Pakistan Army's operational capacity was increased as well. The successive governments in Pakistan, allocated substantial resources for modernisation of the Army despite financial constrains.

The new units and regiments were raised during the Bhutto period. Gen Zia came to power through a coup in July 1977, made efforts in enhancing the combating capacity of the Army. Whoever came to power in Pakistan made endeavours to expand and modernise the Army.

The modernisation process of the Army began during the Bhutto period that was continued by the successive regimes. The trend was intensified during the Zia period because of the flow of the US/West weapons and funds to Pakistan in the 1980s. As flow of the weapons to Pakistan increased, the strength of the Army grew. In the post-1988 scenario, modernisation process of the Army continued and its strength increased. The Military Command and Control Systems were restructured, post-1971.

## Modernisation of the Army during Bhutto

Zulfiqar Ali Bhutto became President on 20 December 1971, in place of Gen Yahya Khan. Bhutto assumed Presidency while Pakistan was in the days of gravest crisis.[1] The loss of East Pakistan deeply hurt Pakistan and caused unprecedented fears and resentments. Fears were expressed at home and abroad about the fragmentation of the residual Pakistan. Pakistan military was psychologically broken and demoralised. The sense of pride was severely injured because of the military debacle and the loss of East Pakistan. Bhutto became Prime Minister on 14 August 1973 and Fazal Illahi Chaudhury was elected as the President by the National Assembly and the Senate. Bhutto retained defence portfolio and appointed a Minister of State for Foreign Affairs and Defence, Aziz Ahmad, to undertake business not appropriate for a Prime Minister. With retaining two important portfolios, defence and foreign affairs, enabled Bhutto in restructuring the military and setting the direction of foreign policy. Bhutto took various measures, including military restructuring, to enhance security of the country.

In the post-1971 war scenario, Pakistan had been facing serious challenges. The loss of East Pakistan, revival of Pakhtunistan issue[2], and Baluchistan insurgency, brought Pakistan under tremendous pressure. India's high defence expenditure and arms procurement in the period was considered in Pakistan, as threats to its security. Moreover, India's 'peaceful nuclear explosion' in May 1974, alarmed Pakistan. India's defence expenditure witnessed a steady rise during 1972-77. The manpower of the Indian Army was not increased but witnessed increase in the mobility and strike capability of the infantry, artillery and armoured units. Defence production was increased. India continued to receive sophisticated weapons and military hardware from abroad, particularly from the Soviet Union. Pakistan noticed the development and made efforts to strengthen its military.

---

[1] Bhutto assumed the offices President and Chief Martial Law Administrator on 20 December 1971. He continued with martial law until 21 April 1972 when an Interim Constitution (1972) was enforced. Gen Yahya declared martial law on 25 March 1969 that continued till 21 April 1972. Bhutto mover over to Prime Ministership on 14 August 1973 when parliamentary system was introduced under the 1973 Constitution. Fazal Illahi Chaudhury was elected President.

[2] The new government in Afghanistan formed under the leadership of Sardar Mohammad Daud in 1973. Sardar Mohammad Daud replaced Zahir Shah through a coup in July 1973 and revived the Pakhtunistan issue, and launched a massive anti-Pakistan propaganda.

Bhutto removed several senior military officers from service in the first four months (December 1971-April 1972) of assumption of power, like Lt Gen Gul Hassan Khan, Chief of Army Staff, and Air Marshal Rahim Khan, Chief of Air Staff, who were removed in March 1972. Some major changes were introduced in the administrative structure of the military high-command:

1. The nomenclatures of the heads of the three Services were changed from the C-in-C of the Army, the C-in-C of the Navy, and the C-in-C of the Air Force to the Chief of Army Staff, the Chief of Navy Staff, and the Chief of Air Staff respectively. The three chiefs were brought under the command of the Joint Chiefs of Staff Committee, with the President of Pakistan as the Commander-in-Chief. This system encouraged close cooperation among the three Services and stressed joint responsibility for planning, direction, and the conduct of war.

2. The tenure of the Chiefs of Staff was initially fixed at four years, but later, in 1975, it was reduced to three years. The government also decided not to give extension to the Services Chiefs.[3]

3. The post of Chairman of the Joint Chiefs of Staff Committee (JCSC) was created on the permanent basis, in order to promote the integrated defence system. Gen Mohammad Shariff was appointed its first Chairman on 1 March, 1976.

4. A *White Paper on Higher Defence Organisation* was issued by the Government of Pakistan in May 1976. It outlined the defence and strategic policy of the government and institutional arrangements to deal with defence affairs. The *White Paper* urged the integrated defence approach with the ultimate responsibility of the Prime Minister.

5. The Naval headquarters were established at Karachi at the time of birth of Pakistan whereas the Army and the Air Force headquarters were situated at Rawalpindi and Peshawar respectively. The Naval

---

[3] This principle was not applied after Zia's military intervention in July 1977. A number of senior officers, including Services Chiefs, were granted extensions.

headquarters were shifted to Islamabad in 1974, to facilitate greater cooperation between the three services and civil administration. The Air Force headquarters were also shifted to Rawalpindi in 1983.

The 1973 Constitution (enforced on 14 August 1973) clearly outlined the role and function of the military. The military was required to "defend Pakistan against external aggression or threat of war, and subject to law, act in aid of civil power when called upon to do so." [4] Bhutto discouraged the Army involvement in day-to-day affairs of the country. But the continued disturbances and insurgency in Baluchistan allowed the Army to play an important role in maintaining internal security. The Army was drawn in maintaining internal security although it was in transition.

In the 1971 war, Pakistan lost East Wing and India held its forces as the Prisoners of War (POWs). India held 90,000 POWs. Some 70,000 were military, and others were civil servants, military dependants, and private individuals. Absorbing the returnees was problematic for the Pakistan Army. Some did not wish to continue to serve and some were pensioned off. Others were not suitable, mentally and physically, to undertake military duty. However, the Army managed the transition. The strength of the Army was maintained at about 300,000, including 25000 Kashmiri troops recruited in their eponymous area and to all intents and purposes, regular soldiers. The loss of the East Wing had little effect on recruitment, as there had been few Bengalis in the Army, but it did have considerable effect on the economy of Pakistan.

Bhutto issued a *White Paper on Higher Defence Organisation* in May 1976, that gave the Prime Minister ultimate authority, relating to defence and national security. A Defence Committee of the Cabinet (DCC) would assist the Prime Minister in his deliberations, while a defence council headed by the Defence Minister would implement the DCC's decisions.

Pakistan had been facing serious economic crisis. Bhutto thought that he would achieve growth by economic reforms and nationalisation. But he did not get expected results. Despite all problems, defence expenditure rose during the Bhutto period. Table 1. demonstrates defence expenditure

---

[4] *The Constitution of the Islamic Republic of Pakistan, 1973*, Article 245

during the Bhutto period. Defence expenditure witnessed a steady rise in the 1970s as expected. Bhutto allocated substantial amount of resources for defence in order to increase defence capability. The Bhutto government allocated more resources to the military than any previous government.

## Defence Expenditure 1971-77

| Year | In Million Rupees | Percentage of the Total Government Expenditure |
|------|-------------------|------------------------------------------------|
| 1971-72 | 3725.5 | 59.09 |
| 1972-73 | 4439.6 | 59.34 |
| 1973-74 | 4948.6 | 42.02 |
| 1974-75 | 6914.2 | 42.83 |
| 1975-76 | 8103.4 | 46.00 |
| 1976-77 | 8120.6 | 44.71 |

Source: Hasan-Askari Rizvi, *The Military and Politics in Pakistan 1947-86* (Delhi: Konark Publishers, 1988), p.205

**Table: 1**

These resources were spent on the modernisation and expansion of the three services as well as for removing hardship of the officers and other ranks. The Army received a large chunk of the resources for its modernisation and expansion. The Pakistan Army was grown during the Bhutto period, in both manpower and weapons.

The Bhutto government paid attention for indigenous production of arms and ammunitions. A Defence Production Division was established in the Ministry of Defence in 1973, to encourage defence production. The existing ordnance complex at Wah was expanded and modernised and three new ordnance factories were established at Sanjwal, Gadwar, and Havailian. The Mechanical Tool Factory at Landi and the Heavy Mechnical Complex at Texila began supplying military orders.

The Bhutto government received weapons from abroad. Pakistan could not afford to choose its suppliers since it possessed the US/West-oriented defence systems. Pakistan was dependent on the US and Europe for weapons. President Nixon partially lifted embargo on arms sale to Pakistan, that was imposed during the 1971 war, on 14 March 1973. Military sales were resumed on a case-by-case basis. India protested to the US about the resumption of defence cooperation with Pakistan, particularly as it involved training as well as supply of weapons. The US supplied arms to Pakistan but those were in small quantity. However, quality was much superior.

The US decision to lift embargo on supply of arms to Pakistan and India, in February 1975, facilitated the obtaining of arms from the US. The US embargo on arms sales was first imposed during the India-Pakistan War of 1965. Later, it was imposed during the India-Pakistan War 1971. The lifting of arms embargo in 1975 provided an opportunity to Pakistan to obtain new weapons. First, Pakistan's defence system was US-oriented and depended on the US. Therefore, Pakistan was hit harder by the US denial to supply arms. Second, Pakistan's indigenous defence production was far below its requirements. China had been providing military assistance to Pakistan but the US and European systems required services that Pakistan possessed. Pakistan received weapons from China and other countries during this period.

The Pakistan Army's strength increased from 278,000 to around 400,000 during the Bhutto period (1972-77) and defence expenditure surged immediately after the war. In 1971-72, the strength of the Army was 356000 that rose to 400000 by the end of the Bhutto government. The Pakistan Army's strength reduced to 278000 in 1972-73 because of the loss of East Pakistan in 1971. But the loss was filled with recruitment of new personnel. The Pakistan Army recruited manpower in large numbers and filled the shortage.

**Pakistan Army's Strength 1971-77**

| Year | Army | Navy | Air Fore |
|:---:|:---:|:---:|:---:|
| 1971-72 | 365000 | 10000 | 17000 |
| 1972-73 | 278000 | 10000 | 17000 |
| 1973-74 | 300000 | 10000 | 17000 |
| 1974-75 | 365000 | 10000 | 17000 |
| 1975-76 | 365000 | 10000 | 17000 |
| 1976-77 | 400000 | 11000 | 17000 |

Source: *The Military Balance*

**Table: 2**

The Army continued to recruit personnel to fill the gap that appeared due to loss of East Pakistan. But strength of the Air Force and Navy remained static during the Bhutto period as Table 2. shows. In 1976-77, only 1000 were added to the Navy. Pakistan was dependent on the Army for its managing of internal security. Pakistan's overdependence on the Army created imbalance in forces in the country.

The Pakistan Army increased its units and divisions during the Bhutto period. In 1971-72, the Pakistan Army was organised with two armoured divisions, 12 infantry divisions, one armoured brigade, and one air defence brigade that rose to two armoured divisions, 14 infantry divisions, two independent armoured brigades, one air defence brigade, and five Army aviation squadrons by 1977.[5] The growth of the Pakistan Army was notable during the Bhutto period despite numerous challenges.

## Gen Zia: Expansion and Modernisation of the Army

The Zia rule began in July 1977 and lasted till August 1988. In these eleven years, the Army grew from 400000 to 450000 and its inventory of equipment increased in both quantity and quality. The outlook of the Army changed.

---

[5] *The Military Balance 1971-72, The Military Balance 1976-77*

The Army was weakened, especially at the beginning of Zia's regime and in the early 1980s since officers were required to be involved in martial law.[6] Many good officers were forced to be involved in carrying out administration of martial law in addition to normal military duties. The Army began to lose direction because chain of command became imprecise and unclear. The Army had a chief who was also President, and Zia had to concentrate on running the country. As a result, his attention was divided.

With the Soviet intervention in Afghanistan in 1979, Pakistan's security came under cloud. The conflict in the region provided an opportunity to Pakistan to increase its defence capacity. The three services benefited greatly from the funds and weapons that began arriving in the early 1980s. The Western/US flow of funds and weapons to Pakistan did not only help in strengthening the combating capacity of the Pakistan Army but also enhanced the Pakistan Air Force and Pakistan Navy capacity. The Pakistan Army required the large resources, since its involvement in the conflict was greater. As a result, the Pakistan Army's strength grew during the Zia period. The Pakistan Army's strength was 400000 in 1977-78 that rose to 450000 by 1987-88. The number of infantry divisions, infantry brigades and armoured brigades increased as well. It witnessed an increase in numbers of tanks, APCs and surface-to-surface missiles. Pakistani officers, once again, got opportunities in the US, for briefings, training, and visits concerned with the use of weapons and intelligence.

With acquisitions of tanks from the US and China, the Pakistan Army formed more armoured regiments. Pakistan also stressed on indigenous production of small arms under licence and manufacture of ammunition.

---

[6] Brian Cloughley, *A History of the Pakistan Army: Wars and Insurrections* (Karachi: Oxford University Press, 2006), p. 241

**Pakistan Army's Strength 1977-88**

| Year | Army | Navy | Air Force |
|---------|---------|-------|-----------|
| 1977-78 | 400000 | 11000 | 17000 |
| 1978-79 | 400000 | 11000 | 18000 |
| 1981-82 | 420000 | 13000 | 17600 |
| 1983-84 | 450000 | 11000 | 17600 |
| 1984-85 | 450000 | 11000 | 17600 |
| 1985-86 | 450000 | 15200 | 17600 |
| 1987-88 | 450000 | 13000 | 17600 |

Source: *The Military Balance*

**Table: 3**

The increase of manpower and weapons had an impact on the dilution of the quality of the officers who were being inducted, particularly in the standard of the education. The Pakistan Military Academy (PMA) increased its intake but had to lower its standards in quality of instructors and the educational standard of the entrants. Expansion of the Army meant much more than a mere increase in quantities of the advanced weapons. The Army required more officers and soldiers.

Many of the new entrant to the PMA at Kakul had little knowledge of English language. Zia's emphasis on Urdu language and induction of religious teachings in the Army, further perpetuated the problem. Pakistan received arms during the Zia period which were of western origin and their training manuals were also in English. As a result, insufficient training affected operability. The quantitative and qualitative expansion of the Army required the formation of the new corps headquarters. The three new corps headquarters were formed during the Zia period.

The Zia regime allocated huge resources for development and modernisation of the Army. Defence expenditure saw a steady rise during the Zia period. The flow of funds from the US/West and some Gulf countries enabled Pakistan to allocate huge defence budgets. The funds were required for purchasing the new weapon systems and to meet other expenses. Moreover, huge defence budget enabled the Pakistan Army to recruit manpower.

### Defence Expenditure 1977-88

| Year | In Million Rupees | Total Expenditure | Percentage of the Total Government Expenditure |
|---|---|---|---|
| 1977-78 | 9674.5 | 22781.9 | 42.46 |
| 1978-79 | 10167.6 | 29851.8 | 34.06 |
| 1979-80 | 12654.8 | 34845.1 | 36.31 |
| 1980-81 | 15300.1 | 39215.7 | 39.01 |
| 1981-82 | 18630.7 | 43102.5 | 43.22 |
| 1982-83 | 23224.0 | 67617 | 34.34 |
| 1983-84 | 26798.0 | 75902 | 35.30 |
| 1984-85 | 31794.0 | 91151 | 34.88 |
| 1985-86 | 35120.0 | 129230 | 27.17 |
| 1986-87 | 38619.0 | 152110 | 25.38 |
| 1987-88 | 47015.0 | - | - |

Source: Hasan Askari Rizvi, *The Military and Politics in Pakistan 1947-86* (Delhi: Konark Publishers, 1988), p. 244; Ayesha Siddiqa Agha, *Pakistan's Arms procurement and Military Buildup 1979-99: In Search of a Policy* (New York: Palgrave, 2001), p. 80

**Table: 4**

Defence expenditure never declined from 1977 to 1988 as Table 4 shows. It continued to rise during the Zia period. Zia used the funds to enhance the quantity and quality of the weapons that were required for the Army. Armoured artillery and infantry were improved both in quantity and quality. The new regiments were formed. The Pakistan Army was organised with two armoured divisions, 14 infantry divisions, three independent armoured brigades, three independent infantry brigades, two additional brigades, and five Army aviation squadrons in 1977-78 that rose to two armoured divisions, 17 infantry divisions, four independent armoured brigades, eight independent infantry brigades, eight artillery brigades, three additional artillery brigades, six armoured recce regiments, and one special services group, by 1988.[7] Indeed, it was a big improvement in the Army.

## Benazir Bhutto and Nawaz Sharif and the Army

The Army grew during the civilian rules as well. The civilian governments allocated resources for development and modernisation of the Army, including two other services. The Army obtained substantial amount of resources for its modernisation programme. Defence expenditure witnessed a steady rise during the civilian governments and never came down as Table 5 demonstrates.

### Defence Expenditure 1988-99

| Year | In Million Rupees | Total Expenditure | Percentage of the Total Government Expenditure |
|------|-------------------|-------------------|-----------------------------------------------|
| 1988-89 | 51053.0 | | |
| 1989-90 | 58708.0 | | |
| 1990-91 | 64623.0 | | |
| 1991-92 | 75751.0 | | |
| 1992-93 | 87461.0 | | |
| 1993-94 | 91776.0 | | |
| 1994-95 | 100221.0 | | |
| 1995-96 | 119658.0 | | |
| 1996-97 | 127400.0 | | |
| 1997-98 | 1338.00.0 | | |
| 1998-99 | 145000.0 | | |

Source: Ayesha Siddiqa-Agha, *Pakistan's Arms Procurement and Military Buildup 1979-99: In Search of a Policy* (New York: Palgrave, 2001), p. 80

**Table: 5**

[7] *The Military Balance 1977-78, The Military Balance 1987-88*

The Pakistan Army's strength increased between 1988-89 and 1998-99. The recruitment in the Pakistan Army was continued in this period. The strength of the Army was 450000 in 1988-89 that rose to 520000 by 1998-99. Table 6 demonstrates substantial increases in the strength of the Army between 1988-89 and 1992-93. The strength of the Army rose from 450000 to 515000 by 1993. The Pakistan Army added 65000 only in the five years. There were two responsible factors in rising the strength of the Army in this period - the withdrawal of the US/West forces from the region and India-Pakistan tensions.

### Pakistan Army's Strength 1988-99

| Year | Army | Navy | Air Force |
|------|------|------|-----------|
| 1988-89 | 450000 | 16000 | 17600 |
| 1989-90 | 480000 | 15000 | 25000 |
| 1990-91 | 500000 | 20000 | 30000 |
| 1992-93 | 515000 | 20000 | 45000 |
| 1993-94 | 510000 | 22000 | 45000 |
| 1994-95 | 520000 | 22000 | 45000 |
| 1995-96 | 520000 | 22000 | 45000 |
| 1996-97 | 520000 | 22000 | 45000 |
| 1997-98 | 520000 | 22000 | 45000 |
| 1998-99 | 520000 | 22000 | 45000 |

Source: *the Military Balance*

### Table: 6

The strength of the Pakistan Army did not only increase in this period but also the other two services' strength grew. It is noteworthy that the strength of the Pakistan Air Force increased substantially, in this period. The Pakistan Air Force's strength was 17600 in 1988-89 that rose to 45000 by 1999. However, the Pakistan Navy did not improve in this regard and rose to 22000 by 1999.

In 1988-89, the Pakistan Army was organised with two armoured divisions, 17 infantry divisions, four independent armoured brigades, eight independent infantry brigades, eight artillery brigades, three additional artillery brigades, six armoured recce regiments, and one special services group that rose to two armoured divisions, 19 infantry divisions, seven engineers brigades, one area command (division), three armoured recce regiments, seven independent armoured brigades, one SF group, nine artillery brigade groups, one additional command, and 17 squadrons by 1999.[8] The Pakistan Army needed weapons and manpower to meet the growing security challenges since the US/West forces had been gradually withdrawn from the region and also due to continued India-Pakistan tensions.

## The Musharraf Regime

Gen Musharraf, Army Chief-cum-President tried to improve the Army at every level. He allocated resources for development and modernisation of the Army. It is noteworthy that defence expenditure continued to increase during the Musharraf period. Table 7. shows a steady rise in defence expenditure.

**Defence Expenditure 1999-2008**

| Year | In Million Rupees | Total Expenditure | Percentage of the Total Government Expenditure |
|------|-------------------|-------------------|------------------------------------------------|
| 1999-2000 | 150400.0 | 709100.0 | 21.20 |
| 2000-01 | 131200.0 | 717900.0 | 18.27 |
| 2001-02 | 149300.0 | 826300.0 | 18.06 |
| 2002-03 | 159700.0 | 898100.0 | 17.78 |
| 2003-04 | 180400.0 | 923600.0 | 19.53 |
| 2004-05 | 211700.0 | 1117000.0 | 19.00 |
| 2005-06 | 242000.0 | 1401800.0 | 17.26 |
| 2006-07 | 249900.0 | 1675500.0 | 14.91 |
| 2007-08 | 27500.0 | 1874700.0 | 14.66 |

Source: Pakistan Economic Survey

**Table: 7**

[8] *The Military Balance 1988-89, The Military Balance 1998-99*

The Pakistan Army's strength grew during the Musharraf period although it was not substantial. The strength of the Pakistan Army was 520000 in 1999-2000 that rose to 550000 in 2000-01. Nonetheless, the strength of the Army did not grow after 2000-01 and remained static as Table 8. shows. The Pakistan Army's strength grew to 550000 in 2000-01 because of the Army involvement in operations against the insurgents/ terrorists in the FATA and NWFP. The September 2001 tragic incident in the US compelled Pakistan to start operations against the terrorists in the FATA and NWFP.

**Pakistan Arm's Strength 1999-2009**

| Year | Army | Navy | Air Force |
|---|---|---|---|
| 199-2000 | 520000 | 22000 | 45000 |
| 2000-01 | 550000 | 22000 | 40000 |
| 2001-02 | 550000 | 25000 | 45000 |
| 2003-03 | 550000 | 25000 | 45000 |
| 2003-04 | 550000 | 25000 | 45000 |
| 2004-05 | 550000 | 24000 | 45000 |
| 2005-06 | 550000 | 24000 | 45000 |
| 2006 | 550000 | 24000 | 45000 |
| 2007 | 550000 | 24000 | 45000 |
| 2008 | 550000 | 24000 | 45000 |
| 2009 | 550000 | 22000 | 45000 |

Source: *The Military Balance*

**Table: 8**

The Pakistan Air Force's strength did not grow in the Musharraf period and remained static. However, the strength of the Pakistan Navy fluctuated. The strength of the Navy was 22000 in 1999-2000 and rose to 24000, in 2008. Table 8. shows that the Air Force and Navy are smaller in size than the Army. The flow of funds and weapons from the US/Europe to Pakistan in the post-September 2001 helped in increasing combating capacity of the Army. Sophisticated and technologically advanced weapons flew from the US to Pakistan in this period. The US supplied few arms to Pakistan in the 1990s because the two countries did not have a warm relationship.

Pakistan did not enjoy a warm relationship with the US in the 1990s as a result of which, it received few arms from the US. But Pakistan's relation with the US improved in the post-September 2001 situation and the US arms transfer began in Pakistan. Again Pakistan assumed significance for the US/West. Pakistan had been receiving weapons not only from the US but also China, Ukraine, Belarus, Russia and other countries. The Pakistan Army rose to two armoured divisions, one mechanised independent brigade, 19 infantry divisions, seven engineers brigades, one area command (division), three armoured recce regiments, seven independent armoured brigades, one SF group, nine artillery brigade groups, one additional command, and one aviation (VIP) squadrons, 10 helicopter squadrons by 2008.[9] The combating capacity of the Army increased during the Musharraf period.

## Structure of Army Units

The Pakistan Army is divided into two main branches - Arms and Services. The Army requires these branches to perform efficiently and effectively. The armoured, artillery and infantry are being developed and modernised. The Air Defence, Army Aviation and Signals are being modernised as well. Services are also required for the functioning of the Army. The Army requires services and supports in its performing functions.

---

[9] *The Military Balance 2008*

**Services Supporst**

| Arms | Services |
|------|----------|
| 1. Armoured | 1. Army Service Corps (ASC) |
| 2. Artillery | 2. Army Medical Corps |
| 3. Infantry | 3. Ordnance |
| 4. Air Defence | 4. Electrical and Mechanical Engineers (EME) |
| 5. Army Aviation | 5. Military Intelligence |
| 6. Engineers | 6. Army Education Corps |
| 7. Signals | 7. Army Clerical Corps |
| 8. Aviation | 8. Military Police Corps |

source: *http://en.wikipedia.org/wiki/pakistan_Army*

**Table: 9**

## Command Structures

Prime Minister Zulfiqar Ali Bhutto began to restructure military command and control system to overcome the shortcomings that the military had been facing. Provisions were made in the 1973 Constitution of the country, for restructuring military command and control system. Article 243 (1) of the 1973 Constitution bestowed all military related powers on the Prime Minister. The Commander-in-Chiefs (C-in-C) of the three services, re-designated as Chief-of-Staffs, now came under the control of the Prime Minister. This system was further amended in 1988, placing the President as Supreme Commander. All decisions were to be taken and endorsed by the Cabinet Committee for Defence (DCC), which represented the core of the structure and decision-making mechanism. The DCC dealt with all the issues and was chaired by the head of the government. The diagrams 1, 2 and 3 show the military new command and control system, the Army command and control structure, and the Joint Chiefs of Staff Committee (JCSC) respectively.[10]

---

[10] Ayesha Siddiqa-Agha, *Pakistan's Arms Procurement and Military Buildup 1979-99: In Search of a Policy* (New York: Palgrave: 2001), pp. 35-54

The Chief of the Army Staff (COAS), formerly called the Commander-in-Chief (C-in-C), operates from Army headquarters, Rawalpindi. The Principal Staff Officers (PSOs) that assist the COAS in his duties at the Lieutenant General level, include a Chief of General Staff (CGS) under whom the Military Operations and Intelligence Directorates function - the Chief of Logistics Staff (CLS), the Adjutant General (AG), the Quarter-Master General (QMG), the Inspector General of Training and Evaluation (IGT&E), and the Military Secretary (MS). A major reorganisation in GHQ was done in September 2008, under Gen Ashfaq Parvez Kayani, when two new PSO positions were introduced: the Inspector General, Arms and the Inspector General, Communications and IT, thus raising the number of PSOs to eight.[11] The headquarters function also includes the Judge Advocate General (JAG), and the Comptroller of Civilian Personnel, the Engineer-in-Chief of the Corps of Engineers who is also head of Military Engineering Service (MES), all of them also report to the Chief of the Army Staff. The diagram 1. depicts the military command and control system.[12]

## Military: Command and Control System

**Diagram: 1**

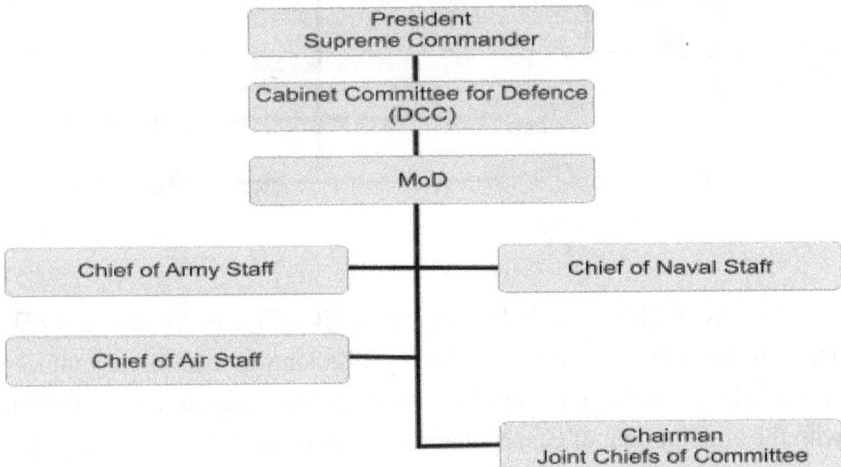

---

[11] Iftikhar A Khan, "Kayani Shakes up Army command", *Dawn*, 30 September 2008
[12] Siddiqa-Agha, n. 10, p.39

among the three services. The diagram 2. shows the Pakistan Army's command and control system in which the Chief of Army Staff is at the top.[13]

# Army: Command and Control

**Diagram: 2**

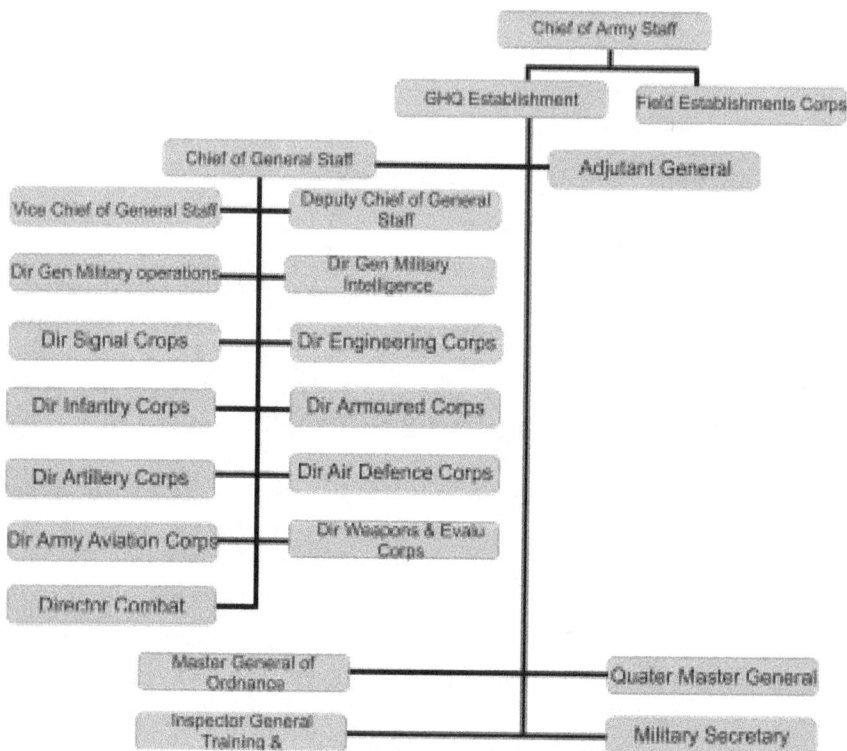

The Joint Chiefs of Staff Committee (JCSC) was created in 1973. The main objective for creation of this organisation was to promote jointness and coordination of all three services. Actually, the JCSC came into function with the appointment of Gen Mohammad Sharrif as its Chairman, in 1976 that provided Pakistan an integrated inter-service mechanism for the higher direction of war. The 1965 and 1971 wars witnessed lack of coordination

---

[13] Ibid, p. 49

among the three services. As a result, Pakistan felt the need to create the JCSC for proper and adequate coordination for future wars.

The Chairman of the Committee is a four-star general and his responsibility includes planning for war during peacetime and giving joint direction during war. In war like situations, the JCSC will assume responsibilities, as the Principal Staff Officer, to assist the government in the supervision and conduct of war.[14] He does not command troops and the only military personnel under him, are his staff. Moreover, he carries out coordination with all inter-services organisations like the ISI and the Pakistan Ordnance Factories. The Chairman is not authorised to interfere in the day-to-day running and direction of the Armed Forces. This action has curtailed the power and influence of the JCSC. It is primarily responsible for preparing joint strategy plans and providing strategic direction to the Armed Forces. Periodically, it reviews size, shape and the role of the three services and advises the government on related aspects of national security and defence.

However, it plays an important role in arms procurement. It is responsible for processing weapons requirements in the light of the overall strategic plans that are made at the joint staff headquarters. The diagram 3. shows the JCSC structure.[15]

---

[14] *http://www.globalsecurity.org/wmd/world/pakistan/jcsc.hmt*
[15] Siddiqa-Agha, n. 10, p. 47

## Joint Chiefs of Staff Committee (JCSC)

**Diagram: 3**

Chairman

Director-General(Joint Staff)

Director (Operations) — Director (Plans)

Director (Intelligence) — Director (Training)

Director (Collaboration) (With friendly countries) — Director (Administration)

Director (Logistics) — Director (Quartering)

Inter-Servieces Organisations

Inter-services Intelligence — Pakistan Ordnance Factories

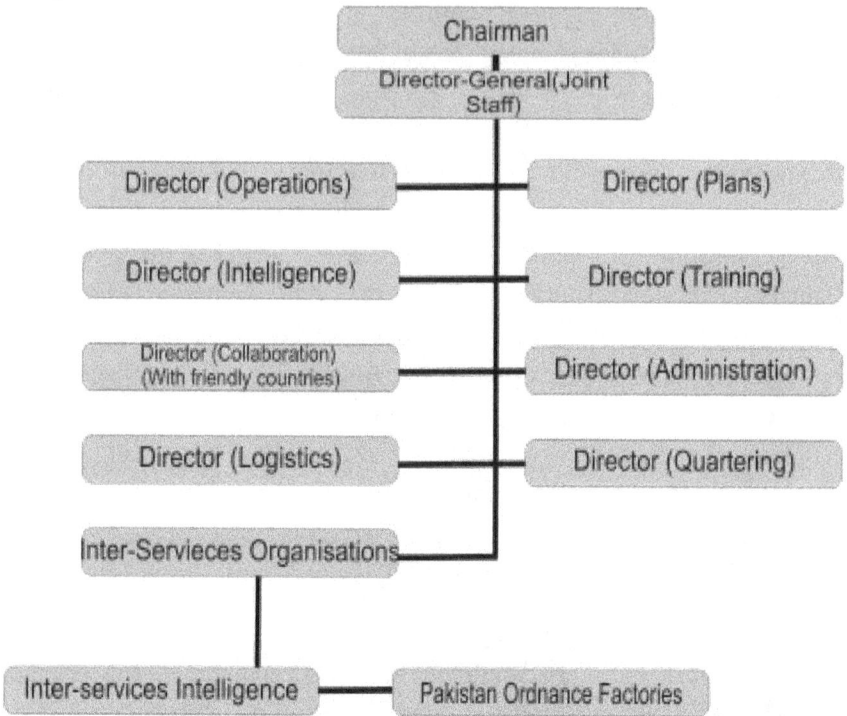

The JCSC could not perform its tasks due to a variety of reasons. Zulfiqar Ali Bhutto's continued dependency on the Army in maintaining internal security and the subsequent coup in July 1977, were major reasons. Gen Zia's coup, after creation of the JCSC in 1976, thwarted all efforts at joint military planning and assigning an equal status to all three service chiefs. After the July 1977 coup, the representation of the three services at the JCSC meetings had become unbalanced. Since the Army chief could not attend the meetings because he had become the President, the Vice-Chief of the Army staff represented him at the organisation. The Army deliberately discouraged the strengthening of the JCSC.[16] This organisation could not achieve its objectives for which it was created. The growing political influence of the Army curtailed the role of the JCSC in carrying out its prescribed tasks.

---

[16] Ibid, pp. 61-62

## Operational Commands

The Army operates six tactical commands during peace time. Each command is headed by General Officer Commanding-in-Chief with the rank of Lieutenant General. Each command is directly affiliated to the Army HQ in Rawalpindi. The diagram 4. shows the structure of operational commands during peace time.[17]

# Operational Commands

## Diagram: 4

```
                        ┌─────────────┐
                        │  Army HQ    │
                        │ Rawalpindi  │
                        └─────────────┘
```

| Punjab Strike Corps Command Rawalpindi | Punjab Holding Corps Com Lahore | Sindh Command Karachi | Kashmir Command Rawalpindi | Western Command Quetta | Strategic Command Rawalpindi |
|---|---|---|---|---|---|

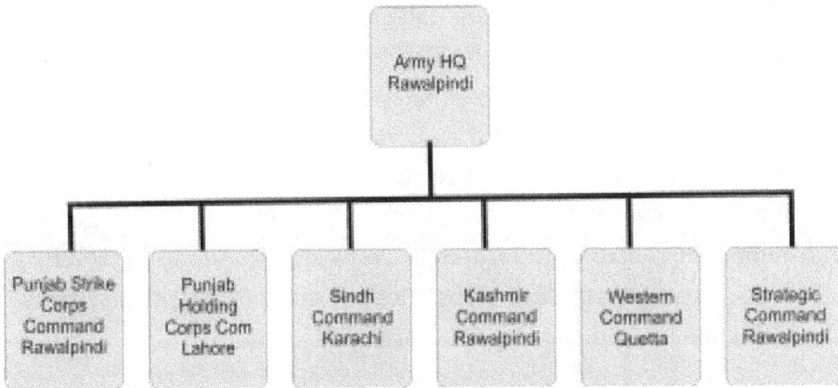

The Punjab Strike Corps Command (Rawalpindi) operates under I Corps (Mangla) and II Corps (Multan). The Punjab Holding Corps Command controls IV Corps (Lahore) and XXX Corps Gujranwala. Sindh Command (Karachi) controls V Corps (Karachi). Kashmir Command (Rawalpindi) controls X Corps (Rawalpindi). XI Corps (Peshawar) and XII Corps (Quetta) operate under the Western Command. Strategic Command controls Strategic Corps (Rawalpindi) and Army Air Defence Command (Rawalpindi).

The Army has divided the entire country into three offensive zones. The Pakistan Army has three offensive formations – Army Reserve North (ARN), Army Reserve South (ARS), and Army Reserve Central (ARC).

---

[17] *http://en.wikipedia.org/wiki/Pakistan_Army*

Each offensive formation supervises a number of corps. The Army Reserve Central (ARC) is under process of formation and is not fully operational.

## Pakistan Army's Corps Commands

The formations and reorganisations of corps commands are important processes in the modernisation of the Army. The Pakistan Army, for the first time, formed I Corps headquarters at Abbotabad (which is now at Mangla) in 1958. It formed the IV Corps at Lahore, Punjab in 1966. The II Corps was formed at Multan, Punjab in 1971, while East Pakistan was in revolt.

The 1971 military fiasco and the emergence of Zulfiqar Ali Bhutto, brought many changes in the realm of military. The military was reorganised and restructured. Bhutto took keen interest in modernising the Army. The Pakistan Army was reorganised and restructured and the new units and divisions were raised. The three corps headquarters were formed during the Bhutto period: V Corps at Karachi in Sindh in 1975, X Corps at Rawalpindi in Punjab in 1974, and XI Corps at Peshawar in the NWFP in 1975. The formations of three corps in a short span of time, reflect Bhutto's determination in strengthening the Army

**Pakistan Army's Corps Commands**

| Corps | HQ Location | Major Formations under Corps | Commander | Notes |
|-------|-------------|------------------------------|-----------|-------|
| I Corps | Mangla, Azad Kashmir | 6th Armoured Division (Kharian), 17th Infantry Division (Kharian, 37th Infantry Division (Gujranwala) | Lt Gen Nadeem Ahmad | Formed 1958; Abbotabad, now is in Mangla; Fought in 1965 and 71 wars, as well as sent replacements to Kashmir for LOC. |
| II Corps | Multan, Punjab | Ist Armoured Division (Multan), 14 Infantry Division (Okara) | Lt Gen Sikandar Afzal | Formed 1971; while East Pakistan was in revolt |
| IV Corps | Lahore, Punjab | 10th Infantry Division (Lahore), 11th Infantry Division (Lahore) | Lt Gen Ijaz Ahmed Bakhshi | Formed 1966: after retirement of Gen Musa Khan as C-in-C |
| V Corps | Karachi, Sindh | 16th Infantry Division (Pano Akil), 18th Infantry Division (Hyderabad), 25th Mechanised Division (Malir) | Lt Gen Shahid Iqbal | Formed 1975; 16, 18 IDs. IDs' are mechanised. It has a lot of independent Brigades as well, since it has all of Sindh to cover. |
| X Corps | Rawalpindi, Punjab | Force Command Northern Areas (Gilgit), 12th Infantry Division (Murree), 19th Infantry Division (Mangla), 23th Infantry Division (Jhelum) | Lt Gen Tahir Mahmood | Formed 1974 |
| XI Corps | Peshawar, North West Frontier Province | 7th Infantry Division (Peshawar), 9th Infantry Division (Kohat) | Lt Gen Muhammad Masood Aslam | Formed 1975 (7, 9): presently engaged in fighting in the Federally Administered Tribal Areas |

| XII Corps | Quetta, Baluchistan | 33rd Infantry Division (Quetta), 41st Infantry Division (Quetta) | Lt Gen Khalid Shameem | Formed sometime in 1984-85 (33, 41) |
|---|---|---|---|---|
| XXX Corps | Gujranwala, Punjab | 8th Infantry Division (Sialkot), 15th Infantry Division (Sialkot) | Lt Gen Nadeem Taj | Formed 1986-87; Each division has 4 brigades and an armoured division is in the process of raising |
| XXXI Corps | Bahawalpur, Punjab | 26th Mechanised Division (Bahawalpur), 35th Infantry Division (Bahawalpur), 40th Infantry Division (Okara) | Lt Gen Muhamm-ad Yousaf | Formed 1986-87 |

Source: *The Military Balance 2008, pakistanidefence.com, Wikipedia.org*

**Table: 10**

The coup in July 1977 and the military's ascendency to power strengthened the military in general and the Army in particular. The Soviet intervention in Afghanistan in 1979, changed the geopolitics of the region. Gen Zia took advantage and expanded and modernised the Army. The three corps headquarters were formed during the Zia period: XII Corps at Quetta, in Baluchistan in 1984-85, XXX Corps at Gujranwala, in Punjab in 1986-87, and XXXI Corps at Bahawalpur, in Punjab in 1986-87. The formations of three corps demonstrate the sensitivity of the government to its security. The new corps headquarters were formed to manage the new units and regiments that were raised during the Zia period. With formations of the new corps headquarters and induction of the new weapons, the combating capacity of the Army increased.

The formations of the new corps commands demonstrate the growing combating capacity of the Army. The corps commands were formed thus-two in the Ayub era, one in the Yahya rule, three in the Bhutto period, and three in the Zia regime. The formations of corps headquarters reflect that the Army grew considerably during the Ayub, Bhutto and Zia rules. The arms acquisitions from abroad helped in the formations of the new corps commands. The formations of corps headquarters show an increasing offensive and defensive capacity of the Army.

The strength of the Pakistan Army is 550000, is organised into Nine Corps Headquarters with Two armoured divisions, 19 Infantry Divisions, Nine Independent Infantry Brigades, Seven Engineer Brigades, Twenty two Independent Brigades (seven armoured, six mechanised, nine infantry), Artillery Nine (corps brigades) and Five brigades, Seventeen Aviation Squander (seven aircrafts, eight helicopters, one VIP, one observation flight), and One Air Defence command with Eight Brigades.[18] The Pakistan Army has reached this stage after long endeavours.

## Conclusion

The Pakistan Army has undergone major changes, post-1971. The Army was reorganised and restructured after the 1971 war debacle. Zulfiqar Ali Bhutto brought changes in the Army. Financial constraints and weapons acquisitions were major hurdles in modernising the Army. Pakistan needed funds and weapons for its Army modernisation programme. Zulfiqar Ali Bhutto expanded relations with foreign countries, for arms and funds and the successive regimes continued that. The process of modernisation started by Zulfiqar Ali Bhutto, was continued by the successive regimes. The new regiments, units and corps headquarters were formed, to meet the defence needs.

Developments in 1979, changed the geopolitics of the region. The Soviet intervention in Afghanistan, in 1979, brought opportunity for Pakistan to receive funds and weapons from the US and West. The Army required funds and arms to raise the new units and regiments. The US/West funds and weapons enabled Pakistan to form three new corps headquarters in the 1980s. The Army used this opportunity to strengthen the organisation and enhance its combating capacity.

But the Pakistan Army has been facing some serious challenges. Financial constrains and weapons acquisitions are still major obstacles in its

---

[18] *The Military Balance,* various issues.

modernisation programme. Organisationally, the Army has grown and carries a complex structure. The Pakistan Army has evolved a command and control system and possesses features as developed countries' armies. The Army has divided the country into three offensive zones and each zone controls its respective corps. The Pakistan Army has developed at both organisational and operational levels. However, it still requires modifications and modernisation.

# 4

# Future Arms Procurement, Defence Industry and Capacity Building

The newly created state sought to ensure security through arms acquisitions and external alignment strategy. In order to procure arms, Pakistan began to expand its relations with the West/US. Arms transfers depend on political relationships between the two countries and regional and global strategic environment as well. The Pakistan-US defence pacts in the 1950s facilitated Pakistan to procure arms from the US. The India-Pakistan War 1965 and the US and Britain arms supply embargo on Pakistan had adverse impacts on the Pakistani Armed Forces. Pakistan sought alternate sources and also established defence production factories to fill the requirements of the defence needs.

Pakistan's relation with China began in the 1950s and assumed a degree of confidence by the late 1960s. China supplied arms and ammunitions to Pakistan during the India-Pakistan War of 1965. Pakistan received arms from the USSR in 1968 and other countries as well. Despite alternate sources, Pakistan sought to establish defence production industry to curtail dependency on the US and Britain. As a result, Pakistan started to establish and expand its defence production industry with external assistance like that of China. Pakistan established a number of defence production complexes in the 1970s that expanded in the 1980s though some of them established in the 1950s and 1960s. The armoured, artillery, and infantry were modernised by procuring weapons from abroad and arms production at home.

Pakistan sought alternate sources for procuring arms and ammunitions. It had been facing two major obstacles in procuring arms and ammunitions: reliable arms suppliers and financial constraints. An appropriate and reliable military hardware supplier and financial constraints had been major hurdles for its military modernisation programme. Pakistan had opted for two options, in order to modernise its military. First, Pakistan sought cost-free arms, or financially affordable ones. Second, Pakistan sought that suppliers would provide arms with a credit facility. Pakistan's relations with the US, China and some European countries were framed in the context of potential arms suppliers.

## US Arms Transfers to Pakistan

The core of Pakistan's relation with the US was formed on the basis of arms transfers.[1] The US supplied arms to Pakistan in the 1950s, that helped in its military modernisation drive. By joining the US-sponsored security organisations in the 1950s, Pakistan became its member. The SEATO and the Baghdad Pact/CENTO were joined by other countries. It intended to deter the Soviet Union from any military adventure. As a result, Pakistan received military and economic assistance in the 1950s. The US supplied arms to Pakistan such as Patton tanks and the artillery guns under the defence assistance programme.

The 1965 War exposed defence preparedness of Pakistan. The war was initiated by Pakistan but it could not resist Indian pressure and counter-attacks. The Pakistan Army acquired 24 Huey Cobra attack helicopters from the first American aid package that proved useful during the 1965 War.[2] The Pakistan Army needed such helicopters to play an anti-tank role, in stopping Indian attacks. This procurement increased defensive capability of the Army. It was preferred because it was cheap.

The flow of the US arms to Pakistan did not continue in the 1960s. The US and Britain imposed arms supply embargo on Pakistan in 1965. As a result, the Pakistan-US relation felt discomfort and bitterness in their

---

[1] Hasan-Askari Rizvi, *Pakistan and the Geostrategic Environment* (New York: St. Martin's, 1993), p. 88

[2] Ayesha Siddiqa-Agha, *Pakistan's Arms Procurement and Military Buildup, 1979-99: In Search of a Policy* (New York: Palgrave, 2001), p. 150

relationship increased. Pakistan realised that it could not completely rely on the US for military support and needed to tap other sources. The most significant outcome of the 1965 war was that Pakistan, in the coming years, became increasingly dependent on China for its defence needs.[3] However, Pakistan continued its defence relation with the US.

Under the leadership of Zulfiqar Ali Bhutto, defence and foreign policies had undergone a change. Pakistan's relations with the US deteriorated because of Bhutto's policies - nuclear, Pakistan-China ties, expansion of Pakistan's relations with Muslim countries, and human rights abuses. However, development in the region, in 1979, eased relations between Pakistan and the US. Therefore, 1979 can be considered as a watershed year in Pakistan-US relations, since Washington reversed its earlier policy. The US offered an aid of $3.2 billion to Pakistan that comprised military and economic assistance programmes. Military received US $1.6 billion to procure hardware for its Armed Forces. Pakistan received US military and economic aid till 1988. With the beginning of the withdrawal of the Soviet Union from Afghanistan in 1988, the US curtailed military and economic assistance to Pakistan.

Pakistan and the US had found a common ground for security alignment in the 1980s, that was a short-lived. This alignment provided economic and military aid to Pakistan. The US supplied arms to Pakistan that enabled Islamabad to start operations against the Soviet troops in Afghanistan. Prior to 1979, Pakistan was not so important because of the peripheral state in the US security interests, abuse of human rights, and nuclear proliferation.

The involvement of the US in Pakistan in the 1980s was primarily to counter the Soviet threat. President Reagan had sought a clear strategic gain over the Soviet Union. The presence of the Soviet bases in South Yemen and Ethiopia, and the loss of Iran, a strong ally in the Persian Gulf, were perceived by the policy-makers in Washington as a reduction in US military capability. Pakistan used this opportunity to justify its requests for procuring military hardware. The US supplied weapons in bulk to Pakistan in the 1980s, that helped in modernising the Army. Pakistan did not get all

---

[3] R S N Singh, *The Military Factor in Pakistan* (New Delhi: Lancer, 2008), p. 357

the arms demanded but most of them were obtained. The US arms transfers to Pakistan increased its firepower, mobility and technological capacity. Pakistan Army's main focus was to improve the armoured and artillery divisions.

**Pakistan-US Arms Transfers**

| Year of Order | Year of Delivery | Weapon Designation | Type | Quantity |
|---|---|---|---|---|
| 1970 | | M-113 | APC | 300 |
| 1981 | 1983/1984/-1985/1986 | BGM-71A TOW | ATM | 1005 |
| 1981 | 1982 | M-48-A5 | MBT | 100 |
| 1981 | 1983/1984 | M-109-A2 155mm | SPH | 32/32 |
| 1981 | 1982 | M-110-A2 203mm | SPH | 40 |
| 1978 | | M-113-AI | APC | 40 |
| 1981 | 1984 | M-88-AI | ARV | 35 |
| 1981 | 1984 | M-901 TOW | APC | 24 |
| 1981 | 1983 | Model 209 AH-IS | Helicopter | 10 |
| 1982 | | M-110-A2 203mm | SPH | 36 |
| 1982 | 1984 | Model 209 AH-IS | Hel | 12 |
| 1982 | 1984/1985 | M-109-A2 155mm | SPH | 18/18 |
| 1985 | 1986/1987/-1988/1989 | M-109-A2 155mm | SPH | 88 |
| 1985 | 1986/1987 | M-113-A2 | APC | 110 |
| 1981 | 1984/1985/-1986 | M-198-155mm | TH | 75 |
| 1985 | 1987/1988/-1989 | BGM-71C 1-TOW | ATM | 2030 |
| 1985 | 1985 | FIM-92A Stinger | Portable SAM | 100 |
| 1986 | 1987 | Model 204 UH-IB | Helicopter | 3 |
| 1987 | | M-198-155mm | TH | 60 |
| 1985 | 1987/1988/-1989 | AN/TPQ-37 | Tracking Radar | 4 |
| 1987 | | BGM-71D TOW-2 | ATM | 2386 |

| 1987 | 1987 | FIM-92A Stinger | Portable SAM | 150 |
|------|------|-----------------|--------------|-----|
| 1988 |      | M-109-A2 155mm | SPH | 20 |
| 1988 | 1996 | M-198 155mm | TH | 24 |
| 1988 | 1989 | AN/TPQ-36 | Tracking Radar | 5 |
| 1989 |      | M-113-A2 | APC | 400 |
| 1990 | 1996 | AN/TPQ-36 | Tracking Radar | 4 |
| 1990 |      | Model 209 AH-IS | Helicopter | 10 |
| 1989 | 1990/19-91 | M-113-A2 | APC | 775 |
| 1990 |      | BGM-71A TOW | ATM | 80 |
| 2001 |      | S-70/UH-60 Blachhawk | Helicopter | 6 |
| 2001 | 2002 | Bell-205/UH-IH | Helicopter | 5 |
| 2002 |      | AN/FPS-88 | Air Sur radar | 6 |
| 2004 |      | Bell-205/UH-IH | Helicopter | 40 |
| 2004 |      | Bell-209/AH-IF | Combat Helicopter | 40 |
| 2004 | 2004-2-005 | Bell-412EP | Helicopter | 26 |
| 2003 |      | L-88 Lass | Air surv radar | 6 |
| 2004 |      | AN/TPS-77 | Air surv radar | 6 |
| 2004 |      | BGM-71 TOW | ATM | 2014 |
| 2005 |      | SA-316B Alouette-3 | Light helicopter | 2 |
| 2005 |      | M-109A5 155mm | SPH | 115 |
| 2005 |      | AN/TPS-77 | Air Surv radar | 6 |

Source: *Stockholm International Peace Research Institute (SIPRI) The Military Balance*

**Table: 1**

The Pakistan Army procured two types of American anti-tank wire-guided missiles – TOW and the TOW-2 – in the 1980s in order to make the helicopters effective. The US sold around 5000 TOW and the TOW 2 anti-tank missiles to Pakistan in the 1980s. But the US stopped transferring these anti-tank missiles after passing the Pressler Amendment in October 1990.

The Pakistan Army sought to improve its infantry. By the end of the 1970s, infantry was dependent upon the G-3 and MP-5 rifles. The G-3 was an old item. The Army needed to procure shoulder-fire missile systems to counter the growing Soviet threat. The acquisition of the American FIM-92A 'Stingers' was needed, to enhance firepower capability of the Army.

Developments in 1979, in the region, brought the opportunity for Pakistan to obtain such systems from the US. Pakistan acquired FIM-92A 'Stingers' both directly and indirectly from the US. Pakistan obtained around 250 FIM-92A 'Stingers' between 1985 and 1987. The US supplied FIM-92A 'Stingers' in large quantity to Afghan *Mujahideen* but only one-third of the systems had reached their destination and the rest were siphoned off. It is a high probability that the stolen systems were inducted into the Pakistan Army. But it cannot be said that all stolen systems were retained by the Army. However, the Pakistan Army retained the missiles in large numbers. The Afghan Mujahiddin sold the stingers at the black market in Pakistan, particularly in the two provinces, NWFP and Baluchistan. The Pakistan Army was involved in diverting the weapons.

The Pakistan Army procured second-hand/refurbished but cheaper tanks like M-48-A5s in 1982. The US military categorised the old tanks as 'excess stock' which were sold to Pakistan at the reduced rate. These tanks were preferred to the M-60s and M1A1s, which were more expensive. The procurement of the M-48-A5s added to Pakistan's existing inventory of similar tanks, as received in the 1960s. There was a plan to establish an overhaul and rebuild facility for the M-48A5s but could not materialise due to enactment of the Pressler Amendment.

The Soviet troops withdrawal from Afghanistan and its disintegration reduced Pakistan's strategic relevance for the US. The US stopped assistance to Pakistan after passing the Pressler Amendment in October

1990. Pakistan never thought of such a scenario. It could not understand the fragile nature of Pakistan-US security linkage and impacts on the US policy-making that deemed suddenly, with the withdrawal of the Soviet troops from Afghanistan. This action was resented by the Pakistani Armed Forces and resulted in deteriorating ties between Pakistan and the US.

The Brown Amendment was passed in 1995 that permitted transfers of certain weapons and spare parts to Pakistan, excluding the F-16s. Nonetheless, the September 2001 tragic incident in the US changed the direction of the Washington-Islamabad relationship. The US involvement in the region surged and Pakistan assumed strategic significance for the US/West. The US attacked Afghanistan and overthrew the Taliban regime. So, as the US presence in the region increased, its involvement in Pakistan grew. The US supplied Bell-205/UH-IH helicopters in 2004 and AN/FPS-88 air surveillance radars in 2002. Pakistan received BGM-71 TOW anti tank missiles in 2004 and M-109A5 155mm self propelled guns in 2005, from the US.

### Europe and USSR/Russia Arms Transfers to Pakistan

Pakistan received arms and ammunitions from Britain, France, Italy, and other European countries. Britain supplied guns and other arms to the Pakistan Army in the 1950s. The flow of arms to Pakistan did not continue in the 1960s as was in the 1950s. As a result, the Pakistan Army had faced difficulties during the 1965 War. The US and Britain arms supply embargo on Pakistan in 1965, created challenges for the Pakistani Armed Forces. Pakistan sought alternate sources for obtaining arms. The USSR supplied tanks, guns and vehicles to the Pakistan Army in 1969.[4] The USSR arms supply to Pakistan did not go well in Washington. Despite the US reservation, the USSR supplied Mi-8 helicopters for the Pakistan Army in 1970-71.[5] However, the Pakistan-USSR arms deal remained for a short period.

France supplied arms to Pakistan in the 1970s. France has served as one of Pakistan's favourite options for arms acquisition since the early 1970s. Pakistan received arms and systems from France mainly for its Air

---

[4] *Stockholm International Peace Research Institute (SIPRI) Yearbook 1969-70*, p. 348; R S N Singh, *The Military Factor in Pakistan* (New Delhi; Lancer, 2008), p. 358

[5] *SIPRI Yearbook 1972*, p. 136

Force and Navy. France supplied the few arms for the use of the Pakistan Army. Italy was also a source that supplied arms to the Pakistan Army. Pakistan received M-47 Patton tanks from Italy in 1968. However, Italy offered limited weapons, particularly sub-systems and components. Italy supplied arms primarily to two smaller services, the Navy and Air Force.

Pakistan received weapons and systems from Sweden, Romania and Austria in the 1980s, for its Army. Sweden supplied approximately 1200 shoulder-fired missiles like RBS-70 to Pakistan, between 1986 and 1987. Pakistan received from Sweden, 100 missiles, as Completely-Built-Unit (CBU). These missiles were integrated for use with Sweden's fire control radar 'Giraffe', procured for assembling at Margalla Electronics in 1986. Pakistan's weapons acquisition drive has increased the combating capability of the Army.

Pakistan started to look to the European arms market in the 1990s, where its choices were France and Britain with whom Pakistan had past experience of arms transfers. These were the sources from which weapons could be purchased without any political conditions imposed by the suppliers. However, the acquisitions were limited because of high prices of weapons.

**Europe and USSR/Russia Arms Transfers to Pakistan**

| Suppliers | Year of Order | Year of Delivery | Weapon Designation | Type | Quantity |
|---|---|---|---|---|---|
| Italy | 1968 | | M-47 Patton | Tank | 3 |
| USSR | | | 130 mm guns | | 200 |
| USSR | 1968 | 1969 | T-54/55 | Tank | 100 |
| USSR | 1968 | 1969 | 130 mm guns | | 200 |
| Turkey | | | Patton | Tank | 100 |
| USSR | | 1970-71 | Mil Mi-8 | Helicopter (Army Aviation Wing) | |
| France | 1977 | | SA-330L Puma | Helicopter | 35 |
| Romania | 1982 | 1983 | SA-316B | Helicopter | 4 |
| Sweden | 1983 | 1986 | RBS-70 | Portable SAM | 400 |

| Sweden | 1985 | 1986-2004 | RBS-70 | Portable SAM | 800 |
|--------|------|-----------|--------|--------------|-----|
| Austria | 1987 | | GHN-45 155mm | TH/TG | 200 |
| Britain | 1987 | | EH-101 | Helicopter | 2 |
| France | 1988 | 1989/1990/-1991 | Rasit-3190B | Surveillance Radar | 6 |
| Britain | 1990 | | Shorland S-55 | APC | 24 |
| France | 1991 | 1994 | Mistral | Portable SAM | 50 |
| Belarus | 1996 | 1997/1998/-1999 | AT-11 Sniper/9M119 | ATM | 5760 |
| Russia | 1995 | 1996 | Mi-17 Hip-H | Helicopter | 12 |
| Ukraine | 1996 | 1997/1998/-1999 | T-80UD | MBT | 320 |
| Russia | 2001 | 2002 | Mi-17/Hip-H | Helicopter | 12 |
| Russia | 2001 | 2002 | Mi-17/Hip-H | Helicopter | 4 |
| Russia | 2003 | 2004 | M-8/Mi-17/-Hip-H | Helicopter | 12 |
| Ukraine | 2000 | 20004-2005 | 5TDF | Diesel engine (AV) | 80 |
| Ukraine | 2002 | | 6TD | Diesel engine (AV) | 315 |

Source: *Stockholm International Peace Research Institute (SIPRI) Yearbook; The Military Balance*

**Table: 2**

Pakistan received weapons from France after 1988. France supplied Rasit-3190B surveillance in 1989, 1990 and 1991, to Pakistan. France also supplied Mistral portable surface-to-air missile in 1994, to Pakistan. France imposed embargo on arms sales to Pakistan, in July-August 1999, in the wake of the India-Pakistan Kargil conflict. The embargo was extended after a military coup in October 1999. Pakistan received arms from Britain, including frigates and some second-hand equipment.

Pakistan sought to procure foreign tanks to fill the shortage. It was not easy to get tanks from abroad. Pakistan approached various countries for this purpose, among which the most significant was Poland, followed by Ukraine and Russia. Initially, the contract was negotiated with Poland for 230 T-72s in 1992. Army Chief Gen Asif Nawaz Shuja was interested in the deal. But the deal was cancelled at the final stage. The cancellation of the deal coincided with the sudden death of Army Chief Gen Asif Nawaz Shuja in January 1993. Despite the Army's need for tanks, the contract was cancelled at its final stage, soon after the death of the Army chief. It reflects the influence of the Army Chief, in arms procurement decisions.

After cancellation of the deal with Poland, Pakistan soon negotiated a deal with Ukraine for T-80UD tanks that were superior to Poland's T-72s. Finally, Pakistan signed a deal with Ukraine for T-80UD tanks in 1996. Ukraine supplied 320 T-80UD tanks to Pakistan in 1997 and 1998. Ukraine supplied around 80 older tanks to Pakistan and did not fulfil the agreement. Some of the components of these T-80UD tanks were being made in Russia. Moscow did not release the components of the T-80UD tanks. As a result Ukraine could not fulfil the contract.

The Eastern part of Europe is a potential source for Pakistan's arms acquisitions. But Pakistan is unable to expand and maintain its relations with the Eastern European countries. In Pakistan's strategic calculus, Eastern Europe is not significant. However, Eastern Europe can be seen as a potential source for Pakistan's arms acquisitions. Pakistan has bought tanks from Ukraine, for its Army. Belarus supplied anti-tank missiles to the Pakistan Army in 1997, 1998 and 1999. For Pakistan, Ukraine and Belarus have emerged as potential sources for procuring tanks for its Army.

**Pakistan-China Arms Transfers**

Pakistan had been receiving hardware arms from China since the 1960s. China provided arms to Pakistan as a policy to strengthen militarily its ally.

Pakistan's arms acquisitions facilitated in modernising the Pakistan Army. The first consignment of around 800 T-59 tanks, arrived in Pakistan in 1965-66 and these tanks started to replace US M-47/M-48 tanks as the Army's main battle tanks.[6] In 1964, China had offered an interest-free loan to Pakistan worth US $ 60 million. Pakistan received an interest-free loan from China worth US $ 40.6 million in 1969, part of which was used to establish the heavy mechanical complex. China offered a loan to Pakistan worth US $ 217.4 million when Gen Yahya Khan visited Beijing, in November 1970. It is noteworthy that this aid to Pakistan was interest-free, and the weapons were free of cost.

China supplied T-59 tanks in bulk, to Pakistan, in the 1970s. After the India-Pakistan War 1971, China became the main source of tank suppliers to Pakistan. The Heavy Industries Taxila (HIT) had begun to overhaul and rebuild the Chinese T-59 tanks in 1979-80. These tanks helped in strengthening the armoured corps, but they were technologically inferior. Pakistan pursued strategy to purchase arms in bulk from China. This policy helped Pakistan in expanding its defence industrial base. Pakistan bought weapons in large quantity from China and they were overhauled and rebuilt at home. Pakistan was the largest single recipient of Chinese military assistance in the 1970s.

---

[6] Singh, n. 3, p. 358

### Pakistan-China Arms Transfers

| Year of Order | Year of Delivery | Weapon Designation | Type | Quantity |
|---|---|---|---|---|
| | 1966-1968 | T-59 | MBT | 100 |
| | 1970 | T-59 | MBT | 100 |
| | 1971 | T-54/55 | MBT | 110 |
| 1973 | 1974 | T-59 | MBT | 159 |
| 1975 | 1978 | T-59 | MBT | 50 |
| - | 1979 | T-59 | MBT | 50 |
| - | 1980 | T-59 | MBT | 50 |
| - | 1981 | T-59 | MBT | 50 |
| - | 1982 | T-59 | MBT | 75 |
| - | 1983 | T-59 | MBT | 75 |
| - | 1984 | T-59 | MBT | 75 |
| - | 1985 | T-59 | MBT | 75 |
| - | 1986 | T-59 | MBT | 75 |
| - | 1987 | T-59 | MBT | 75 |
| - | 1988 | T-59 | MBT | 75 |
| 1988 | 1988/1989/1990 | Hong Ying-5 | Portable SAM | 300 |
| | 1989 | T-59 | MBT | 75 |
| 1989 | 1990 | T-69 | MBT | 20 |
| 1988 | 1989/1990/1991 | T-69 | MBT | 275 |
| 1990 | 1991 | M-11 Launcher | SSM | 20 |
| 1990 | 1991 | M-11 | SSM | 55 |
| 1989 | 1991 | Khalid | MBT | 10 |

| 1988 | 1989/1990 | HN-5A | Portable SAM | 200 |
|------|-----------|-------|--------------|-----|
| 1989 | 1990/1991 | Red Arrow-8 | ATM | 100 |
| 1990 | 1992/1993/199-4/1995/1996 | T-85-IIAP | MBT | 282 |
| 1989 | 1990-2004 | Red Arrow-8 | ATM | 15100 |
| 1993 | 1994-2004 | QW-1 Vanguard | Portable SAM | 850 |

Source: *Stockholm International Peace Research Institute (SIPRI) Yearbook; The Military Balance*

**Table:3**

The nature of the Pakistan-China relationship underwent a change after 1979. The Pakistan-China ties focussed more on military technology transfers and arms production cooperation. This coincided with Chairman Mao's departure from the political scene. Post-1979, China stressed on economic development and started economic reforms. In this period, economic rather than political considerations became more relevant to the Chinese policy-makers. This was a period when China's relation with the US had begun to become less hostile as well as those with India. There was no substantial improvement in ties between India and China but New Delhi wanted to maintain friendly relations with Beijing. With visit of India's Foreign Minister Atal Bihari Vajpayee to China in 1979, India-China relations began to improve. The India-China relations improved to a degree in the 1980s that the two countries decided to disengage some troops from their borders. Prime Minister Rajiv Gandhi's visit to China in 1988, was a part of the process of normalisation of relations between the two countries. At the invitation of Premier Li Peng, India's Prime Minister Rajiv Gandhi paid an official visit to China on 19-23 December 1988.[7] The developments in the 1980s had a direct impact on Pakistan-China ties.

---

[7] *http://www.fmprc.gov.cn/eng/ziliao/3602/3604/t18017.htm*

After 1979, China no longer considered it necessary to supply free arms to Pakistan, although these weapons were relatively cheaper than the weapons that were acquired from the US/West, by Pakistan. China asked Pakistan to pay for supply of military hardware. Moreover, Pakistan had to pay interest for the credit given by China, for weapons purchase. Pakistan also found it increasingly difficult to negotiate the price of weapons systems, with Chinese manufacturing firms. China started to view Pakistan as a potential source of earning foreign exchange. A qualitative change had taken place in their bilateral ties. The China-Pakistan axis had become slack.[8] China, no longer, vehemently supported Pakistan on the Kashmir issue and did not encourage Islamabad in adopting a confrontational stance against India. China's policy on the Kashmir resolution changed from self-determination to mutual resolution, by both countries. This transformation in policy of China had shed its 'one friend-one enemy' approach for a 'two friends' stance.[9] However, China continued to supply military hardware to Pakistan.

Some Pakistani authors held a different view. Hasan-Askari Rizvi viewed the period beyond 1979, as a continuation of the 1960s' stance.[10] In Rizvi's opinion, there was no change in China's policy towards Pakistan, except on the resolution of the Kashmir issue. He saw no fluctuation in China's policy towards Pakistan and his argument was based on the exchange of high level delegations and similar issues. It is true that the Pakistan-China ties were warm and cordial, even after 1979 and continued that way in the 1990s as well.

The Chinese tanks remained the primary choice for Pakistan that could add to the numbers. China supplied tanks to Pakistan in the 1960s but Beijing supplied tanks in bulk to Islamabad in the 1970s. Pakistan received T-59 in large numbers from China in the 1970s and the trend continued. In the 1980s, China supplied T-59 to Pakistan as well. Pakistan received T-69 tanks from China in 1989 and 1990. China also supplied 282 T-85II tanks to

[8] Siddiqa-Agha, n. 2, p. 107

[9] Raju G C Thomas, *South Asian Security in the 1990s*, Adelphi Paper 278, (London: July 1993), p. 13

[10] Rizvi, n. 1, pp. 148-62

Pakistan between 1992 and 1996. A contract was singed later for the transfer of technology of T-85II.

The Pakistan Army was curious to acquire these tanks, in order to enhance its capability. The Army had thee objectives: to acquire cheap Chinese tanks that can be overhauled, to assemble the Chinese tanks locally with some modifications and upgrades, and to produce indigenous tanks. The process of modifications and upgrades began in 1979 and the T-59 tank was upgraded locally. The T-69 and T-59 tanks were overhauled. After these, the T-85 was upgraded. In 1990, the main battle tank (MBT) known as Al-Khalid was upgraded. China did not only supply T-59 tanks and the MIG fighter aircrafts, but also helped Pakistan to establish the defence production industrial base at Pakistan Aeronautical Complex (PAC) Kamra, the Heavy Industries (HIT), and Heavy Mechanical and Electrical Complexes at Taxila.[11] China's contribution in strengthening the Pakistan Army and expanding its defence industrial base, is notable.

Zulfiqar Ali Bhutto initiated projects for attaining self-reliance in defence systems that was continued by the successive regimes. Gen Zia acquired tanks from China and upgraded locally. This policy was continued by Army Chief Gen Mirza Aslem Beg. The Al-Khalid tank was compared with tanks such as the Russian T-72 and the US M1A1. But it could not be produced due to certain fundamental problems in the local defence industry. The designs of the Chinese T-96 and T-85 tanks were to develop but could not succeed locally.

China supported Pakistan during the Afghan war. Deng Xiaoping and Zhao Zhiyang assured Zia when he visited China in 1982. China supplied military hardware to Pakistan worth US $794 million from 1979 to 1992. China continued military hardware supply to Pakistan, but a paradigm shift in the Chinese policy had taken place. China's military and non-military aid to Pakistan continued to maintain a certain degree of relationship between the two countries. These gestures were only depiction of the cosmetics relationship but not the real policy.

---

[11] Farooq Hameed Khan, "Towards an Everlasting Partnership", *The Nation*, 29 December, 2010

However, China continued to remain the main source of nuclear material and missile technology for Pakistan. Nuclear and missile technology transfers relationship developed in the 1980s. Beijing preferred to supply sensitive material and technology to Islamabad. Pakistan remained one of the biggest buyers of Chinese technology. It is noteworthy that Chinese technology was qualitatively poor and had a limited number of buyers. Pakistan was a buyer like others. The fact cannot be ignored that these sales provided revenue to China.

Pakistan sought to make indigenous shoulder-fired missiles with China's help. The 'Anza' and 'Anza II" were made with Chinese assistance. However, these two shoulder-fired missiles primarily consisted of Chinese subsystems and were assembled in Pakistan. Pakistan launched the ballistic missiles project that produced two systems: Haft I (range 80 km) and Haft II (range 300km). These were developed and test-fired in 1989. Pakistan sought to acquire ballistic missile capability and increase options for nuclear delivery systems. These missiles were primarily based on Chinese materials and technology. Pakistan only assembled these missiles, and all systems were imported from China. Pakistan procured M-11 missiles from China. Its range was 300 km and upgraded to 600 km. It is noteworthy that both Pakistan and China refused to disclose the exact number of missiles transfers. The Chinese M-11 missiles were considered Pakistan's greatest defence against India's 'Prithvi' and 'Agni' missiles. The US criticised transfers of M-11 missiles to Pakistan. The US sought to stop a ballistic missile race in the region and to discourage the transfers of such technology that would enable regional states to deliver nuclear warheads.

China assisted in developing Pakistan's defence production industry. Beijing's assistance was considered vital for developing Pakistan's poor defence industrial resources. In the absence of a sound defence production base in Pakistan, China's weapons transfers played vital role in consolidating the ties between the two countries. China's contribution in developing Pakistan's defence industry is significant.

## Other Sources

Pakistan's other new suppliers are South Africa and North Korea. South Africa supplies systems, sub-systems and components to mainly Pakistan

Air Force and its organisation, the Air Weapon Complex. They are involved in acquiring systems and sub-systems from South Africa. North Korea supplied missiles and missile-related technology to Pakistan.

## Defence Production Industry

Pakistan's indigenous weapons production consists of a variety of projects and activities and most of the major projects started in the 1960s. Ayub Khan initiated some projects but the progress was slow during his period. In fact the defence production projects, in a major way, were started in the 1970s and intensified then onwards. Zulfiqar Ali Bhutto established some defence production industries and expanded the existing projects. Bhutto established a Defence Production Division in the Ministry of Defence in 1972. New projects were also started during the Zia period.

Pakistan's first Prime Minister, Khan Liaqat Ali Khan, issued a directive within four months of the creation of Pakistan, to set up an ordnance factory, in collaboration with British Royal Ordnance to manufacture .303 calibre rifles and its ammunition in Rawalpindi.[12] Liaqat's death delayed the project. But his successor, Khawaja Nazimuddin continued the plans and laid foundation at Wah Cantonment. Actually, the Wah defence complex came into operation in 1954.

However, the decade of 1950s and 1960s did not witness substantial growth of defence production facilities. The suspension of military aid and the arms embargo during and after the 1965 war, on Pakistan, was a major driving factor to go for self-reliance in defence production and also for diversification of the sources of weapons procurement.[13] The US and Britain arms supply embargo on Pakistan in 1965 created problem during the war. Pakistan did not give importance to its domestic defence industry in the early years since it had been receiving arms from the US. Pakistan sought to curtail its arms dependency on external suppliers. In order to curtail its arms dependency on external suppliers, Pakistan began to establish defence production industry. Bhutto took various measures to set up a defence production industry in Pakistan.

---

[12] *http://www.globalsecurity.org/wmd/world/pakistan/wah.htm*
[13] Shalini Chawla, *Pakistan's Military and Its Strategy* (New Delhi: KW Publishers, 2009), p. 124

*Pakistan Ordnance Factories (POFs):* Pakistan Ordnance Factories (POFs) is located in Wah Cantt, Rawalpindi, Pakistan. The POF was set up in 1951 and is the largest defence industrial complex. It is a defence industrial complex, producing conventional arms and ammunition under the Ministry of Defence Production. It produces projectiles, infantry equipment and ammunition, rocket and artillery propellants, carbide, fuses, explosives, steel products, and even military clothing.[14] It produces for three services of the Armed Forces. The POFs also specialise in manufacturing of commercial explosive, hunting ammunition, and possess extensive facilities for the manufacture of brass, copper and aluminium ingots, extrusions and sections for non-military applications.[15] However, the POFs produces weapons for the Army in large quantity. The POFs consists of 14 Factories and seven subsidiaries.[16]

## Factory

- Weapons Factory
- Bombs & Grenades Factory
- Tungsten Carbide Factory
- Machine Gun Factory
- Filling Factory
- Propellants Factory
- Heavy Artillery Ammo Factory
- Small Arms Ammo Factory
- Brass Mill
- Tungsten Alloy Factory
- Tank Ammunition Factory
- Explosives Factory

---

[14] *http://pofwah.com.pk/products.hmt*
[15] http://www.pof.gov.pk/
[16] *http://www.pof.gov.pk*

- Medium Artillery Ammo Factory

- Clothing Factory

## Subsidiaries

- Wah industries Ltd.

- Wah Nobel (Pvt) Ltd.

- Wah Nobel Chemicals Ltd.

- Wah Nobel Detonators Ltd.

- Wah Nobel Acetate Ltd.

- Attock Chemicals (Pvt) Ltd.

- Hi-Tech Plastic (Pvt) Ltd.

The POF produces various items but some are sub-standard and of poor quality. It produces about 70 major items and millions of components for its Armed Forces. The wide range of products include a variety of NATO calibre infantry weapons and ammunition, tank ammunition, air craft and anti-air craft ammunition, artillery ammunition, rockets, air craft bombs, pyrotechnics, mortar bombs and hand grenades, and a number of ordnance and commercial products.[17] The ammunition production units have a capacity worth $ 70 million to produce but operate at a capacity worth $ 30-40 million. It never utilises its full capacity.

The Army GHQ has deputed a thousand inspectors for ensuring quality but there is no improvement in it. The management was unable to introduce any significant research and development in the organisation. Some reverse engineering and minor modifications were carried out during the 1980s, termed as R and D.[18] Factories managed to copy the Russian 100 mm and 75 mm HEAT anti-tank ammunition, and RPG-7.[19] Similarly, the American 73 mm fine-stabilised rocket was modified that was obtained during the Afghan war. The British made 105 mm TK Hesh explosive was copied to

---

[17] *http://www.pof.gov.pk.maboutus.htm*

[18] Siddiqa-Agha, n. 2, p. 119

[19] Ibid,

make the 100 mm explosive. Minor modifications were introduced in the butt of the German G-3 rifle, where the original design was replaced with a retractable butt stock.

The POFs have been engaged in joint ventures with various countries. Initially it started joint ventures with the Royal Ordnance Factories, Britain, in 1951, and established the first plant for production of .303 calibre rifles. A small arms production facility was set up in collaboration with Germany. This was followed by other various joint ventures with China and other countries. Pakistan established its first joint venture abroad with Saudi Arabia at Al Kharg. This facility makes weapons and ammunitions of various types, including G-3 rifles and 7.62 calibre machine guns. The POFs export their products to various countries like Saudi Arabia, Bahrain, Bangladesh, Sri Lanka, UAE, Indonesia, Malaysia, Myanmar, and Cambodia.

***Heavy Industries Taxila (HIT):*** Heavy Industries Taxila (HIT) situated around 35 km north-west of Rawalpindi, near Wah Cantt, was set up with Chinese assistance in the late 1970s. In 1971, a Heavy Rebuild Factory Project was conceived to rebuild Chinese T-59 tanks. The idea was to gradually learn how to produce an indigenous tank. As the fleet of T-59 manufactured by China grew, HRF was set up at Taxila in the late 1970s to undertake rebuilding and modernisation of tanks. The experience acquired in enhancing firepower, mobility and protection, significantly enhanced the capabilities of HRF. Subsequently, the HRF grew into a multi-factory complex. The HIT facility was formerly known as Heavy Rebuild Factory (HRF). It has over 7000 workers.

Until 1960s, Pakistan obtained tanks, initially from the US (M-47 and M-48 Patton class in the 1950s and 1960s), and then from China T-59 and the USSR T-54/55. These tanks required modifications. Overhauling and modifications of the tanks required facilities where it could be performed. Pakistan established the HIT for this purpose. The HIT gradually started to build tanks for the Pakistan Army.

The HIT approach was to modify and assemble foreign technology. A project was launched to make the main battle tank. The idea was to build an indigenous tank on the experience of overhauling and rebuilding Chinese tanks. It was considered as an efficient way to obtain the main battle tank for the Army and would be easier to make because of earlier experience. The design was derived from the combination of existing blueprints of the Chinese T-85 and T-69II.

The facility consisted of five units: two of them were to overhaul/ rebuild the Chinese T-Series and American M-Series tanks; one unit each was involved in the assembly and production of the main battle tank and armoured personnel carrier; and the one unit was to make the gun barrel. The HIT is also a manufacturing facility that has built the Main Battle Tank 2000, known as 'Al-Khalid'. In fact, Al-Khalid is an ensemble, of Chinese components.

The indigenous tank was known as MBT-2000 or Al-Khalid and was to have a 125 mm gun with APFSDS, HEAT and HE ammunition.[20] Additional features included improved armour, an upgraded engine, a laser range finder and a computerised fire control system. The Al-Khalid was planned to use 45 percent components from the previous models and the project was undertaken with Chinese assistance. A deal was signed worth $ 1.2 billion in 1988-89 with the Chinese company NORINCO.[21] The NORINCO had to spend a major portion of the total cost of the project. Under the plan, the tank manufacturing factory was to produce 150-200 tanks annually. The HIT received technologies from China such as shell casting, gas nitriding, and a tool tip plant that was needed for T-59 tanks. Pakistan has overhauled around 1000 T-59 tanks and tank engines.

It was claimed that Pakistan had produced indigenous Al-Khliad tanks. But it was not entirely true. The HIT did not produce all components that were required for Al-Khalid. The HIT did not produce major components. Vital components were imported from foreign sources which led to delay in production. China's defence industry was not supplying good quality electronics. Moreover, this also increased the cost of production. However, the HIT performed limited role in manufacturing the Al-Khalid, and was only to assembly it. There was no sign of minimising dependency, mainly because of defence industrial complex.

---

[20] Ibid., p. 120
[21] *SIPRI Yearbook 1992*, p.344

Another project was launched in 1987-91 with General Dynamics help to overhaul and rebuild M-48A5 American tanks. The M-48A5 tanks were acquired in 1982, from the US, as part of its military assistance programme.[22] The people from the HIT went for training at the M-48 rebuild factory in Arafiya, Turkey. A new factory was set up for this purpose, on the pattern of the T-series tank factory. But the project was stalled with the US imposition of sanction on Pakistan in 1990.

The HIT also produces Armoured Personnel Carrier M-113 and IFV Al-Zarar fighting vehicles, for the Pakistan Army. It produces the cost-effective armoured fighting vehicles, armoured personnel carriers and tank guns. In addition, in-house manufacture of a large array of components required, has been undertaken and an infrastructure for interacting with the indigenous industry, for development of materials and components, has been taken on.

The HIT launched another project to assemble armoured personnel carriers. A deal was signed with the US company FMC in 1989, to assemble 775 completely-knock-down (CKD) kits of the US M113-A2 APCs.[23] However, this project was not completely affected with passing Pressler Amendment in October 1990. But the pace of the work slowed down because of the unavailability of all the kits.

***Institute of Optronics (IOP):*** The Institute of Optronics was established at Rawalpindi, in 1985, to assemble and manufacture the night vision devices for the Armed Forces. The idea was to start from assembly to gradually manufacture the product at home. The Army sought to avoid the procurement of the complete-built-units. The process of assembly was begun in 1988 and the delivery to the Army was made in the same year.

The IOP is involved in production and testing facilities of night vision devices, based on Image Intensifier Tubes. The IOP produces major devices for the Army. It is involved in the assembly of four types of devices for the Army, which are:

1.    AN/PVS-4A (Individual Served Night Vision Weapon Sight)

---

[22] *SIPRI Yearbook 1984*, p. 252
[23] *SIPRI Yearbook 1992*, p. 343

2.  AN/TVS-5A (Crew Served Night Vision Weapon Sight)

3.  AN/PVS-5A (High Performance Night Vision Goggles)

4.  GP/NVB-4A and GP/NVB-5A (High Performance Night Vision Binoculars)[24]

The night vision systems, without turning night into day, vastly improve the ability of the Armed Forces to perform a number of vital functions related to force effectiveness. Command and control, surveillance, movements both tactical and logistical and accuracy of firepower are some of the areas of activities, in which the night vision devices, play a vital role.

***Margalla Electronics (ME):*** The Margalla Electronics was created in 1984 as a self-reliance project under the Defence Production Division, to manufacture radars. The ME was to repair and rebuild electronic equipments, apply research to improve equipment performance and reliability, and modify original design and production.[25] Within a short span of time, the ME acquired sophisticated skills and hardware, necessary for assembling, testing, and repairing of various types of military electronics products.[26] The ME has co-produced and fielded sophisticated state-of-the-art radar systems and communications equipment jointly, with various foreign companies. However, the ME has not produced anything of its own. The ME carries out, primarily, reverse engineering of the cards (computers/electronic chips) of the various systems.

***The Yasoob Truck Project:*** The government made efforts to develop the automobile industry in the 1960s and 1970s but it went in vain. There was no automobile engineering base for the military, by the 1980s. With public and private partnership, a project was undertaken. The Trans-Mobile Ltd (TML) was established that was represented by a semi-government corporation, Pakistan Automobile Corporation Limited (PACO). Since 1990, the PACO is involved in production of defence vehicles, acquisition of foreign

---

[24] *http://www.pakboi.gov.pk*

[25] "Pakistan Military Consortium: Armed Services of Pakistan", *http://www.pakdef.info/ pakmilitary/companies.*

[26] Ibid

technology and investment into the automobile sector in Pakistan.[27] It started

to manufacture trucks for the military. The Army was interested in two types of trucks like 4 x 4 and 6 x 6. The first prototypes for the 6 x 6 and 4 x 4 were approved by the Army in 1991 and 1994 respectively. The Army was involved in testing and inspection of the vehicles. The Army had placed an order for around 3000 trucks delivery in five to six years. No production figures for the Yasoob were officially released. However, it is understood that around 450 (6 x 6) and 250 (4 x 4) were delivered between 1993 and 1995.[28] The local industry has no capability to make certain components, so, major components like engines, gearboxes and so on, were to be imported from foreign. The indigenous input comprised only mechanical engineering and fabrication.

*Missiles and Military Electronics:* The government launched several projects to manufacture missiles and laser range finders such as the Chinese Red Arrow-8 and Swedish RBS-7 in the 1980s. Moreover, work started on an indigenous missile Anza-II. The Kahuta Research Laboratories undertook to manufacture the laser range finder. The LRF 786P laser range finder was described as a medium range, hand held, lightweight and rugged device. Its range was given as within 150 m to 15 km. Various sources claimed that the equipment was made with imported components. The same opinion was also expressed about the missile Anza-II. This shoulder fired anti-aircraft missile has the same specifications as the US FIM-92A stinger and was also made under Abdul Qadir Khan's supervision.

The missiles supposedly produced by Pakistan were actually assembly work with 70-80 percent components imported from China or North Korea.[29] Pakistan produced the Red Arrow-8 anti-tank missile with the Chinese assistance. The Swedish RSB-70 missile was manufactured at the Precision Engineering Complex, Karachi. The RSB-70 missile was procured from Sweden in 1986 in CUB form. Later Pakistan and Sweden signed a deal for transfer of technology. The Swedish missile was basically assembled

---

[27] http://www.ebd.gov.pak/Corporations/PACO/PACO.pdf

[28] "Yasoob (6 x 6) 6000 kg truck (Pakistan), Trucks", *http://www.janes.com/articles/Janes-Military-Vehicles-and-Logistics/Yasoob-6-x-6-6-000-kg-truck-Pakistan.html*

[29] Siddiqa-Agha, n. 2, p. 125.

from imported components. The Precision Engineering performed the mechanical work required for the missile, at Karachi. The Precision Engineering Complex has produced missiles in large numbers.

Pakistan has developed a series of missiles with China and other countries' assistance: Haft series, Ghauri series, Shaheen series, and M-11 (direct import from China). China provided a complete plant in 1995 to Pakistan, to produce M-11 missile and their variants. China provided Haft series and M-11 missiles whereas North Korea provided Ghauri series (originally Nodong) to Pakistan.[30] Pakistan's Shaheen missiles are built and developed with China's assistance. Both China and North Korea have significantly contributed to Pakistan's missile build-up. However, China's role is prominent to Pakistan's missile build-up.

## Conclusion

Pakistan required arms and ammunitions for its defence needs. As a result, it aligned itself with foreign powers. Pakistan signed defence and security pacts with the US, that facilitated in obtaining arms and funds. The flow of the US/West arms to Pakistan, helped in expansion and modernisation of the Army, including Air force and Navy. The Pakistan Army's combating capacity increased with the induction of the US/West arms into it. The flow of the US and Britain arms to Pakistan was disrupted in 1965. As a result, Pakistan sought alternate sources for obtaining weapons.

Pakistan diversified source of arms acquisitions because of the inconsistent US and Britain arms supply policy. The US and Britain arms supply embargo on Pakistan in 1965 had adversely affected its Armed Forces, since it was dependent on their arms supply. As a result, Pakistan approached other countries for weapons. The USSR supplied arms to Pakistan though those were in small quantity. France and Italy supplied arms to Pakistan. The arms flew in bulk to Pakistan from the US, Britain, Sweden, Austria, Romania and other European countries in the 1980s, as a result of the Soviet intervention in Afghanistan, in 1979. In the 1990s, Russia, Belarus and Ukraine supplied arms for the Pakistan Army and continued that. China supplied weapons to Pakistan.

---

[30] *http://www.wisconsinproject.org/countries/pakistan/missiles.html*

China had been consistently supplying tanks and other arms to Pakistan since 1965, that primarily expanded Pakistan's defence industrial base and increased the Pakistan Army's combating capacity. China's assistance is considered vital for developing Pakistan's poor defence industrial resources and technology. In the absence of defence production capability, China's arms transfer to Pakistan became a significant issue in their bilateral ties. China supplied tanks, in bulk, to Pakistan in the 1970s and 1980s, that actually transformed its Army in a major way. China not only transferred arms to Pakistan but also assisted in establishing the defence production industry. Conventionally, India is superior to Pakistan. But the Pakistan Army's combating capacity has increased with acquisitions of arms from abroad. Armoured, artillery and infantry are being modernised with induction of arms from the US/West, China, Russia, Ukraine, Belarus and other countries. Pakistan's arms acquisitions policy has helped in strengthening their Army.

# 5

# Conclusion

The Pakistan Army has grown to over five hundred thousand personnel and has survived successive military stalemates, defeats, the trauma of defeat in 1971, and professional aberration because of repeated military intervention. Gen Ayub started to expand and modernise the Army since Pakistan required a strong Armed Forces, to manage and guard the two active frontiers – eastern and western. The successive regimes in Pakistan paid attention towards it and allocated resources for modernisation of the Armed Forces. The Army received a large chunk of resources for its modernisation. The Pakistan Army had faced numerous challenges in its modernisation process. Financial constrains, shortage of manpower, lack of infrastructure and assets, and unreliable arm suppliers were major challenges that Pakistan had been facing. However, the Pakistan Army had been able to develop and modernise after long efforts.

In the beginning, Pakistan had faced numerous challenges in raising the Army. The newly created state did not have sufficient resources to meet the requirements for raising the new units and divisions. In the process of consolidation, the newly formed state required strong Armed Forces, that could guard and manage its frontiers. Pakistan required funds and weapons for expansion and development of the Armed Forces. Gen Ayub as the Army Chief, Army Chief-cum-Defence Minister, and finally President, nurtured relations with the foreign powers to obtain arms and ammunitions. Pakistan forged strategic alliance with the US/West in the 1950s. Pakistan signed defence pacts with the US and became a member of the West-sponsored security organisations, that facilitated the obtaining of arms. As arms and funds from the US/West flew to Pakistan, the Army began to expand and modernise. The flow of funds and arms from the US/West enabled the Pakistan Army to improve its organisational capacity. In the Ayub period, the Army was reorganised and expanded.

Pakistan's strategy of external alignment paid dividends and helped in expanding and modernising its Army. Pakistan's security and defence pacts with the US played a vital role in transfer of weapons and funds to Pakistan. With induction of the US and West weapons, the combating capacity of the Pakistan Army increased. The Pakistan Army's dependency on the US grew. The effect of the Pakistan Army's over dependency on the US/West arms had been witnessed during the 1965 War, and was severe. The Pakistan Army was required to improve in many ways. Arms and training of officers is needed at every level.

Nonetheless, Pakistan could not maintain its warm relationship with the US and West in the 1960s, as enjoyed in the 1950s. The event of the US and Britain arms supply embargo on Pakistan in 1965, changed the Pakistani Armed Forces in general and the Army in particular. The US attitude towards Pakistan-India War 1965, brought perceptible changes in the Army. Pakistan sought alternate sources and pursued policy to diversify arms suppliers. Pakistan approached various countries for arms and ammunitions.

Pakistan sought alternate sources to curtail its dependency on the US and Britain. Pakistan approached China for military and economic assistance and Beijing extended support. China supplied arms to Pakistan during the 1965 War and after. Russia also supplied arms to Pakistan but that remained limited. The Pakistan Army raised divisions with Chinese assistance. Indeed, the Pakistan Army could raise only two corps by 1968, despite the US/West military and economic assistance to Pakistan.

After India-China War of 1962, India assumed a significant place in the US and West strategic calculus. The US and Britain pursued energetic and extensive relations towards India and the two countries' supplied arms. The US did not only supply arms to India but also extended economic assistance. China's attitude towards Pakistan changed because of India-US/West growing strategic relations, transfer of arms to India, and the US and Britain attitude on the India-Pakistan War 1965. China's attitude further changed with the event of dismemberment of East Pakistan in 1971.

The growing India-US/West cooperation after 1962, the US and Britain arms supply embargoes on Pakistan in 1965 and 1971, and East Pakistan's dismemberment in 1971, completely changed the perception of China, towards Pakistan. The 1971 military debacle was a turning point for Pakistan and China-Pakistan relationship. China extended supports to Pakistan and had been repeatedly assuring Pakistan, since 1971, to maintain its 'territorial integrity'. China kept nurturing a warm relationship with Pakistan. In the process of nurturing a warm relationship, China pursued a strategy of transferring arms, free of cost and extending economic assistance to Pakistan. China supplied arms to Pakistan, free of cost, till 1979. Post-1979, China supplied arms to Pakistan at minimum prices and easy loans. China believed that Pakistan would be able, with Beijing's support, to resist the Indian pressure. For Pakistan, a reliable partner was required for arms acquisitions. Pakistan found a reliable partner like China that had been consistently supplying weapons to Pakistan, though those were inferior.

In the 1970s, China assumed a significant place in Pakistan's arms acquisition policy. China's arms supply to Pakistan, particularly tanks, in the 1970s and 1980s, strengthened the Army. China did not only supply arms to Pakistan but also assisted in establishing the defence industry. The Pakistan Army received the Chinese tanks that expanded its defence industrial base and transformed the Army, though they were not of high quality. China also supplied missiles and missiles related technology to Pakistan. China's arms transfers to Pakistan played an important role in consolidating the ties between the two countries. China's arms transfers to Pakistan indicate the convergence of views between the two countries. The convergence of China-Pakistan views had complicated the regional situation.

Post-1971, the military was restructured. The Army was restructured as well. Bhutto initiated various measures to strengthen the military. The post of the JCSC was created in 1976, but became redundant with the July 1977 coup. Weapons were inducted in the Army during the Bhutto period. Pakistan's foreign policy orientation changed, post-1971 and relations were expanded with foreign countries, to obtain funds and arms. Pakistan's ties with China significantly improved in the 1970s, since Pakistan needed a reliable arms supplier. Bhutto stressed for modernisation of the Army and self-reliance, in defence production.

The comprehensive and substantial growth of the Pakistan Army was witnessed, post-1971 although its foundations were laid down during the Ayub period. China's arms supply to Pakistan, particularly tanks in the 1970s, had strengthened armoured vehicles capability. China also supplied other weapons to Pakistan in this period but the Chinese tanks in the 1970s enabled Pakistan to expand its defence industrial base. China also supplied arms to its artillery and infantry. China continued to supply arms to Pakistan in the 1980s. China's contribution is notable.

Modernisation process was continued in the post-Bhutto period as well. Gen Zia assumed power through a coup in July 1977. As a result, the Army remained an important player in the country. Developments in the region in 1979, brought an opportunity to Pakistan to obtain arms and funds from the US/West. The convergence of the view of the US/West and Pakistan, on the Afghan issue, drew closer, the two sides and Pakistan played an important role in the conflict. The flow of Western/US weapons and funds to Pakistan in the 1980s, played a significant role in modernisation of the Pakistan Army. The Pakistan Army received tanks, guns, missiles, and other weapons in bulk from the US/West in the 1980s, that increased its combating capacity.

Britain and France supplied weapons to the Pakistan Army in the 1970s and 1980s. France supplied SA-330 L Puma helicopter to the Pakistan Army in 1977. In the 1980s, the Western weapons and funds flew in bulk to Pakistan. France, Britain, Sweden and Romania supplied weapons to the Pakistan Army. The phenomenal growth was witnessed in the artillery and infantry in this period. Pakistan received SA 316 B helicopter from Romania, RBS-70 portable surface-to-air missile from Sweden, GHN-45 guns from Austria, and EH-101 helicopter from Britain in the 1980s. As a result, the combating capacity of the Pakistan Army increased.

The US supplied weapons, in bulk, to Pakistan in the 1980s. It supplied tanks, helicopters, guns, stingers and other weapons to Pakistan in this period. Pakistan's armoured, artillery, and infantry improved with induction of the US weapons. Pakistan received FIM-92A Stinger in bulk from the

US, that remarkably improved its infantry. The US supplied BGM-71D TOW-2 tanks to Pakistan that strengthened its armoured vehicles capability. Pakistan received M-110-A2 203mm guns and Model 204 UH-IB helicopters from the US. But the US arms supply to Pakistan did not continue in the 1990s, since the Soviet withdrawal from Afghanistan reduced Pakistan's strategic relevance for the US/West.

In the aftermath of the September 2001, Pakistan again assumed significance for the US and the West and extended military and economic assistance to Pakistan. The US supplied arms to Pakistan in the post-September 2001. The US supplied Bell-205/UH-HI, Bell-209/AH-IF and Bell-412EP helicopters, M-109A5 155mm guns, AN/FPS-88 and AN/TPS-77 air surveillance radars, and BGM-71 A TOW anti-tank missile to Pakistan.

Pakistan received weapons from Russia, Ukraine, and Belarus in the 1990s and onwards. Russia supplied helicopters Mi-17/Hip-H in 1996 and 2002 andM-8/Mi-17/Hip-H in 2004 to Pakistan. Belarus supplied AT-11 Sniper/9M 119 anti-tank missile to Pakistan in 1997, 1998 and1999. Ukraine supplied T-80UD tanks to Pakistan in 1997, 1998 and 1999. Pakistan also received 5 TDF diesel engines, from Ukraine in 2004 and 2005. The flow of weapons from Russia, Ukraine and Belarus to Pakistan, filled the gap that arose in the event of the US arms supply sanctions, against Pakistan, in the 1990s.

China's assistance to Pakistan is considered vital for developing Pakistan's poor defence industrial resources and technology. Pakistan received arms from China in bulk that helped in expanding Pakistan's defence industrial base. China supplied main battle tanks in large quantities, to Pakistan, that increased firepower capacity of the Army. In the absence of defence production capability, China's arms transfer to Pakistan became a significant issue in their bilateral ties. China did not only transfer arms to Pakistan but also assisted in establishing its defence production industry. China's consistent arms supply to Pakistan enabled the Army to increase its combating capacity.

The pattern of interactions between Pakistan and China reflects a complex relationship that the two countries enjoy. China's presence in Pakistan Occupied Kashmir (POK) is a sheer reflection of complex ties between the two countries. The convergence of the China-Pakistan view has complicated the regional situation. China's consistent arms supply to Pakistan and its growing presence in POK, are sources of concern for India. China's policy to strengthen militarily, Pakistan and its physical presence, will have wider ramifications. Pakistan-China nexus and China's military hardware transfers to Pakistan may adversely affect regional security. However, the Pakistan Army can not match with the Indian Army in terms of numbers and otherwise. India has conventional superiority and many advantages over Pakistan.

The Pakistan Army has been facing challenges at its two active frontiers – eastern and western. It is actively involved in operations against terrorists, Taliban, and insurgents at its western frontier. The groups have posed a serious security threat to Pakistan and their actions and activities have raised questions on the survival of Pakistan. They are considered as existential threats to Pakistan. Pakistani society is diverse and divisive. The fissiparous tendencies exist in Pakistan. As a result, Pakistan has been consistently and persistently challenged. The continued internal problems and external threats have created the sense of insecurity in Pakistan. The Army is required to meet defence needs of the country.

The striking capacity of the Pakistan Army has increased and the Army has divided the entire country into three offensive zones. The Pakistan Army has three offensive formations – Army Reserve North (ARN), Army Reserve South (ARS), and Army Reserve Central (ARC). Actually, the third formation, Army Reserve Central (ARC) is in the raising process.

With the 550000 strength, modern and sophisticated arms, missiles, and nuclear delivery capable missiles, the Pakistan Army appears to be emerging as a strong force in the region. With the US, the West, China, Russia, Belarus and Ukraine weapons, the Pakistan Army is being expanded, developed and modernised. The Pakistan Army has acquired modern and sophisticated weapons that are required for combating. The Pakistan Army is being developed and modernised to tackle internal and external challenges. Pakistan has a smaller forces and limited capability but will remain a significant player in the region.

# Bibliography

## Books

Abbas, Hassan, Pakistan's Drift into Extremism: Allah, the Army, and America's War on Terror (New Delhi: Pentagon Press, 2005)

Akhund, Iqbal, Memoirs of a Bystander: A Life in Diplomacy ((Karachi: Oxford University Press, 1997)

Aijazuddin, FS, ed, The White House and Pakistan 1969-74 (Karachi: Oxford University Press, 2002)

Arif, General Khalid Mahmud, Working With Zia: Pakistan's Power Politics 1977-88 (Karachi: Oxford University Press, 2005)

- Khaki Shadows: Pakistan 1947-1997 (Karachi: Oxford University Press, 2001) Aziz, Mazhar, The Military Control in Pakistan: The Parallel State (New York: Routledge, 2008) Bhutto, Benazir, Daughter of The East (London: Simon & Schuster, 2007)

- The Gathering Storm (New Delhi: Vikas Publishing House, 1983)

- Daughter of Destiny (New York: Smon and Schuster, 1989) Burke, SM and Salim Al-Din Quraishi, The British Raj in India (Karachi: Oxford University Press, 1995) Burki, Shahid Javed, Pakistan Under Bhutto, 1971-77 (London: Macmillan Press, 1980)

- Pakistan: The Continuing Search for Nationhood (Boulder: Westview Press, 1991)

- Historical Dictionary of Pakistan (Lanham, MD: The Scarecrow Press, 1999) Burki, Shahid Javed and Craig Baxter, Pakistan Under the Military (Boulder: Westview Press, 1991) Cloughley, Brian, A History of Pakistan Army: Wars and Insurrection (Karachi: Oxford University Press, 1999) Chakma, Bhumitra, Pakistan's Nuclear

Weapons (London: Routledge, 2009) Chawla, Shalini, Pakistan's Military and Its Strategy (New Delhi: K W Publishers, 2009) Cheema, Pervaiz Iqbal, Pakistan's Defence Policy , 1947-58 (Basingstoke: Macmillan, 1990)

-   The Armed Forces of Pakistan (Crowa Nest Australia: Allen and Unwin, 2002) Chishti, Lt Gen Faiz Ali (retd), Betrayal of Another Kind: Islam, Democracy and The Army In Pakistan (Rawalpindi: PCL Publishing House, 1990) Choudhury, GW, The Last Days of United Pakistan (London: C Hurst & Co, 1974) Cohen, Craig, A Perilous Course: US Strategy and Assistance to Pakistan (Washington DC: Centre for Strategic and International Studies, 2007) Cohen, Stephen P, The Pakistan Army 1998 Edition (Karachi: Oxford University Press, 1998) Cohen, Stephen Philip, The Idea of Pakistan (Delhi: Oxford University Press, 2005) Constitution of Pakistan, 1973 (Lahore Mansoor Book House, 1973) Constitution of Pakistan, 1973, With Amendments (Lahore: Mansoor Book House, 1989) Dasgupta, C, War and Diplomacy Kashmir, 1947-48 (New Delhi: Sage Publications, 2002) Faruqui, Ahmed, Rethinking the National Security of Pakistan: The Price of Strategic Myopia (Aldershot: Ashgate, 2003) Feldman, Herbert, From Crisis to Crisis: Pakistan 1962-69 (Karachi: Oxford University Press, 1972)

-   The End and the Beginning: Pakistan 1969-71 (London: Oxford University Press, 1975) Finer, SE, The Man on the Horseback: The Role of Military in Politics (London: Pall Mall Press, 1962 Gauhar, Altaf, Ayub Khan: Pakistan's First Military Ruler (Lahore: Sang-e Meel Publications, 1993) Grare, Frederic, Pakistan and the Afghan Conflict, 1979-85 (Karachi: Oxford University Press, 2003) Habib, Irfan, An Atlas of the Mughal Empire (Delhi: Oxford University Press, 1986) Harrison, Selig S, In Afghanistan Shadows: Baluch Nationalism and Soviet Temptations (Washington DC: Carnegie Endowment for International Peace, 1981) Jalal, Ayesha, The State and Martial Rule: The Origins of Pakistan's Political Economy of Defence (Cambridge: Cambridge University Press, 1990)

-   Democracy and Authoritarianism in South Asia: A Comparative and Historical Perspective ( Cambridge: Cambridge University Press, 1995 Janowitz, Morris, Military Institutions and Coercion in the Developing Nations (Chicago: The University of Chicago Press, 1977) Kamal, Dr. K I, Pakistan: The Garrison State (New Delhi: Intellectual Publishing House, 1982) Kapur, Ashok, Pakistan's Nuclear Development (London: 1987) Kaul, Lt Gen BM, Confrontation With Pakistan (Delhi: Vikas Publications, 1971) Keesing's Research Report 9, :akistan: From 1947 to the Creation of Bangladesh (New York: Keesing's Publications, 1973) Kennedy, Gavin, The Military in the Third World (London: Gerald Duckworth & Co, 1974) Khan, Fazal Muqeem, The Story of the Pakistan Army (Lahore: Oxford University Press, 1963)

- Pakistan's Crisis in Leadership (Islamabad: National Book Foundation, 1973) Khan, Gohar Ayub, Glimpses into the Corridors of Power (Karachi: Oxford University Press, 2007) Khan, Lt Gen Gul Hassan, Memoirs of Lt Gen Gul Hassan Khan (Karachi: Oxford University Press, 1993) Khan, Mohammad Ayub, Friends Not Masters (London: Oxford University Press, 1967) Khan, Saadullah, East Pakistan to Bangla Desh (Lahore: Lahore Law Times Publications, 1975) Kux, Denis, The United States and Pakistan, 1947-2000: Disenchanted Allies (Washington DC: Woodrow Wilson Centre Press, 2001) Looney, Robert E, Third-World Military Expenditure and Arms Production (New York: St Martin's Press, 1988) McKinlar, Robert, Third World Military Expenditure, Determinants and Implications (London: Pinter Publishers, 1989) McMohan, Robert J, The Cold War on the Periphery: The United States, India, and Pakistan (New York: Columbia University Press, 1994) Malik, Abdullah, Fauj aur Pakistan (2) (Army and Pakistan) (Lahore: Kauser Publishers, 1988) Margolis, Eric S, War at the Top of the World: The Clash for Mastery of Asia (Toronto: Key Porter Books, 2001) Menezes, SL, Fidelity & Honour: The Indian Army (New Delhi: Viking, 1993) More, Jr, Raymond A, Nation Building and the Pakistan Army (Lahore: Aziz Publishers, 1979) Mudiam, Prithvi Ram, India and the Middle East (London: British Academic Press, 1994) Musharraf, Pervez, In the Line of Fire (New York:

Free Press, 2006) National Defence College Publication, Islamabad (Islamabad: nd) Nawaz, Shuja, Cross Swords: Pakistan, Its Army and the Wars Within (Karachi: Oxford University Press, 2008) Niazi, Lt Gen AAK, The Betrayal of East Pakistan (Karachi: Oxford University Press, 1998) Pakistan Economic Survey (Government of Pakistan) Pasha, Mustafa Kamal, Colonial Political Economy (Karachi: Oxford university Press, 1998) Rahman M Attiqur, Our Defence Cause (London: White Lion Publishers, 1976)

- Leadership: Senior Commanders (Lahore: Ferozsons, 1973) Riza, Shaukat, The Pakistan Army, 1947-49 (Lahore: Wajidalis, 1984)

- The Pakistan Army, 1966-71 (Lahore: Army Education Press, 1990) Rizvi, Hasan-Askari, The Military and Politics in Pakistan 1947-86 (Delhi: Konark Publishers, 1988)

- Pakistan and the Geostrategic Environment (New York: St. Martin's Press, 1993)

- Military, State and Society in Pakistan (London: Macmillan Press, 2000) Shafqat, Saeed, Civil-Military Relations (Boulder: Westview Press, 1997) Shaikh, Farzana, Making Sense of Pakistan (London: Hurst & Company, 2008) Sherwani, Latif Ahmed, Pakistan, China, and America (Karachi: Council For Pakistan Studies, 1980) Siddiqa-Agha, Ayesha, Pakistan's Arms Procurement and Military Build-up 1977-99: In Search of a Policy (New York: Palgrave, 2001) Siddiqa, Ayesha, Military Inc: Inside Pakistan's Military Economy (London: Pluto Press, 2007) Singh, R S N, The Military Factor in Pakistan (New Delhi: Lancer, 2008) Sirohey, Admiral Iftikhar A, Truth Never Retires (Lahore: Jang Publishers, 2000) Stockholm International Peace Research Institute (SIPRI) Yearbook Tahir-Kheli, Shirin, The United States and Pakistan: The Evolution of an Influence Relationship (New York: Praeger Publishers, 1982)

- India, Pakistan and the United States: Breaking with the Past (New York: Council of Foreign Relations Press, 1997) Talbot, Ian, Pakistan A Modern History (London: Hurst & Company, 2005 Talbott, Strobe, Engaging India,: Diplomacy, Democracy, and the Bomb (Washington

DC: The Brookings Institution, 2004) The Military Balance (London: IISS) Torrens-Spence, Jonny, Historical Battlefield of Pakistan (Karachi: Oxford University Press, 2006) Wirsing, Robert G, Pakistan's Security Under Zia, 1977-88 (New York: St Martin's Press, 1991)

- India, Pakistan, and the Kashmir Dispute (New York: St Martin's Press, 1998) Wise, David and Thomas B Ross, The U-2 Affair (New York: Bantam Books, 1962) Wolpert, Stanley, Roots of Confrontation in South Asia: Afghanistan, Pakistan, India & Superpowers (New York: Oxford University Press, 1982) Young, Tan Tai, The Garrison State (Lahore: Vanguard Books, 2005) Ziring, Lawrence, Pakistan: The Enigma of Political Development (Kent, England: Dawson & Sons, 1980)

- Pakistan: At the Crosscurrent of History (Lahore: Vanguard, 2004

## Newspapers

Dawn The Nation Daily Times Observer The News Jung Nawa-e Waqt Ausaf

## Internet Sites

http://www.globalsecurity.org/wmd/world/pakistan/jcsc.hmt

http://www.en.wikipedia.org/wiki/Pakistan_Army

http://www.fmprc.gov.en/eng/zillao.hmt

http://www.pofwah.com.pk/products.hmt

http://www.pof.gov.pk

http://www.pakdef.info/pakmilitary/companies

http://www.ebd.gov.pak/Corporations

http://www.janes.com

http://www.wisconsinproject.org/countries/pakistan/missiles.html

http://www.pak/Army.com

# Index